Fontana Introduction to Modern Economics
General Editor: **C. D. Harbury**

Each of the seven books in the series introduces the
reader to a major area or aspect of modern
economics. Each stands on its own, but all fit
together to form an introductory course which
covers most A-Level and first year university
syllabuses, and those of most professional bodies.

An Introduction to Economic Behaviour, by C. D.
Harbury, Professor of Economics, City University.

Britain and the World Economy, 1919–1970, by
L. J. Williams, Senior Lecturer in Economics,
University College of Wales, Aberystwyth.

Private and Public Finance, by G. H. Peters,
Professor of Economics, University of Liverpool.

Income, Spending and the Price Level, by A. G.
Ford, Professor of Economics, University of
Warwick.

Economics of the Market, by
G. Hewitt, Lecturer in Economics at
the Civil Service College.

International Trade and the Balance of Payments,
by H. Katrak, Lecturer in Economics, University
of Surrey.

Mathematics for Modern Economics, by R.
Morley, Lecturer in Economics, University of
Durham.

L. J. Williams

Senior Lecturer in Economics,
The University College of Wales, Aberystwyth

Britain and the World Economy, 1919–1970

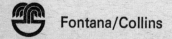 Fontana/Collins

First published in Fontana 1971
Reprinted August 1974

Copyright © L. J. Williams 1971

Printed in Great Britain
for the Publishers Wm. Collins Sons and Co Ltd,
14 St James's Place, London, S.W.1,
by Richard Clay (The Chaucer Press), Ltd,
Bungay, Suffolk

Contents

Introduction

The Book and the Background

This book provides an outline and analysis of Britain's economic development and problems during a time when economic affairs have played a particularly important part. It is intended primarily for students of economics and economic history at A-level, and as background reading for first-year university and professional courses, but it may be read by anyone who wishes to understand Britain's economic problems in their historical and international setting.

The overall objective is to give a broad account of the way in which the British economy and British economic policy have developed since the First World War, and to provide some explanations of these trends. The latter purpose entails the occasional use of economic analysis. For example, the extent to which international effort was directed in the 1920s towards restoring the gold standard system demands a brief explanation of the working of that mechanism. The amount of theory employed is, however, relatively limited, partly because the basic subject-matter—the growth of an economy over an extended period of time—involves one of the less settled areas of economic theory. There is no simple, generally accepted theory of economic growth which can be applied.

Within the Fontana Introduction to Economics series (see list inside the front cover) the book serves as a general background to the volumes which give a closer and more explicit study to economic theory and policy. It is, however, complete itself, though the readers will find that an understanding of general economic principles is an advantage. These are analysed and illustrated for newcomers to the study of economics in the first two volumes of the series: *An Introduction to Economic Behaviour* by C. D. Harbury, and *Private and Public Finance* by G. H. Peters. The theory of international trade and payments is introduced in a more advanced volume, *International Trade and the Balance of Payments*, by Homi Katrak.

Before 1919

1919 is the starting date for this book. But because developments since that date, in both Britain and the world economy, have been substantially affected by what went before, it is necessary to draw attention to a few aspects of the nineteenth-century background. No attempt will be made to provide even the most potted history of the years before 1914: mention will simply be made of a few broad trends. The only basis for the selection of these has been a judgment that they are most relevant to provide a background for the present volume.

Perhaps the most pertinent factor was the substantial dominance of Britain in the international economy for most of the nineteenth century. Britain had long been a major commercial and maritime nation, but her importance in this respect was greatly enhanced when, from somewhere around the end of the eighteenth century, she began to emerge as the first modern industrial nation. Britain's exports of manufactured goods—particularly of textiles and, even more particularly, cotton textiles—rose markedly.

Britain's industrial lead

At the centre of the industrial revolution was the substitution of machinery for handicraft techniques, and the use of new sources of power. Britain, for a wide variety of reasons, took the lead in both these trends. It is important to realise, however, that the widespread application of machinery was initially limited largely to cotton manufacture and that it spread only slowly to other industries. Even by the middle of the nineteenth century a very wide range of production was relatively unmechanised. Where machinery was used, however, it had far-ranging social and economic effects. Thus production tended to become more and more centred in factories. The expense and size of the machinery often made it impossible for manufacturing to be conducted by workers owning their own tools and working at home. Moreover, as steam power gradually replaced an early dependence on water power, these factories were increasingly concentrated in towns. Industrialisation tended to be associated with urbanisation.

Above all, the industrial revolution meant an enormous increase in output because of the more efficient use of resources made possible by the improved technology. Improved transportation played an especially strategic part in enhancing efficiency. The provision of canals and better roads from the second half of the eighteenth century, the spread of a railway network after 1825, and the emergence of the iron steamship all contributed substantially to major reductions in the cost of transport. Markets were dramatically widened; raw materials more easily and cheaply brought together; passengers carried more rapidly and comfortably. The expansion in total output enabled the rising rate of population growth to be sustained and even, in time, permitted the greater numbers to enjoy a higher standard of living. From the higher output also came the savings necessary for the investment of more capital to sustain a future growth of output.

The period of the industrial revolution bristles with unresolved questions. Why did the revolution first occur in Britain? What factor or factors caused the transformation? Did it initially lead to a fall in general living standards? But we need notice only two well-established aspects of the process. First, that it was revolutionary in the sense that it effected a fundamental transformation of society. This was true even during the first half of the nineteenth century when— as has already been indicated—the change was far from complete. Contemporaries had little doubt that they were living in revolutionary times; that for good or ill the technical advances had opened up vast new potentialities. Secondly, there is no doubt that Britain's early start made her, for much of the nineteenth century, easily the world's foremost industrial nation.

The Great Exhibition held in 1851 at the Crystal Palace was a demonstration of this superiority: with a few minor exceptions it was British inventions and achievements that led the field. Even as late as 1870 it is estimated that the United Kingdom was responsible for one-third of the total manufacturing production of the world.[1]

British dominance in trade

Britain's industrial dominance contributed to a parallel pre-eminence in world trade. For some of the basic products of the industrial revolution Britain was, for a time, the only major source. And for a longer period her technical leadership ensured that she should continue as the cheapest source. The basis of this dominance was, however, relatively narrow. In the years around 1870, when British supremacy in world trade was at its height, something like four-fifths of the exports of British manufactures consisted of textiles and iron goods.

1. League of Nations, *Industrialization and Foreign Trade*, 1945, p. 13.

Britain's position as an importer was, in some respects, still more striking. The process of industrialisation pushed Britain more or less inexorably towards becoming a major importer of raw materials and food. Britain's industrial revolution was to a significant extent founded upon cotton textiles, which from the outset automatically involved the importation of raw cotton. Timber was another material of which home supplies were inadequate, although this dependence upon imports considerably ante-dated the industrial revolution.

As the scale of British manufacturing production increased, and as domestic resources were exhausted or became insufficient, imports of raw materials persistently rose—not only for existing products like cotton and timber but for such other materials as wool and iron ore. Moreover, the steady shift of British resources (labour and capital) out of agriculture and into industry, where their relative productivity was higher, meant an increasing reliance upon imported foodstuffs. In 1815, at the end of the Napoleonic Wars, the country was still largely self-sufficient in food. By the 1870s imports accounted for nearly half of the consumption of wheat and flour, and the proportion was increasing. The first trickle of meat imports was evident; and the *per capita* consumption of such imported foods as sugar and tea had risen four-fold since 1815.

Britain was thus both the leading exporter of manufactured foods and the major importer of food and raw materials. Between 1800 and the 1870s British exports increased nearly six-fold and her imports nearly ten-fold. By the latter date Britain was directly involved in nearly one-quarter of all world trade.[2] There was no doubt at all that Britain was not only the dominant industrial nation: she was also easily the largest trading nation.

Invisible trade and overseas investment

The more rapid rate of increase in imports, as compared with exports, meant that Britain normally had a substantial deficit on her external trade. The ways in which this deficit was met highlight some other important aspects of Britain's economic pre-eminence in the nineteenth century. The imports and exports so far mentioned cover only the so-called visible trade, the trade in actual, tangible, material goods. There is also the trade in services, the so-called invisible trade, such as the provision of insurance and shipping facilities for for-

2. A. H. Imlah, *Economic Elements in the Pax Britannica*, 1958, p. 190.

eigners.[3] During the century between the ending of the Napoleonic Wars in 1815 and the outbreak of the First World War in 1914, British businessmen persistently earned substantial and growing sums by acting as insurers and shippers for overseas customers.[4] The earnings from shipping largely reflected the fact that throughout this period Britain never owned less than one-quarter of the total world shipping. From 1870 onwards, the proportion was around two-fifths.

Normally the earnings from trading profits, shipping, and insurance were more than enough to reverse the unfavourable balance on merchandise trade. They were, in any event, reinforced by a growing net inflow of earnings from British investments overseas. The overall British balance on current account was thus almost invariably favourable in the century before 1914. The surplus which accrued to Britain might have raised difficult problems of payment for the rest of the world, problems which would have greatly jeopardised the working of the international economy. Fortunately these were avoided, because Britain's surpluses tended to be offset by new British lending abroad. Britain was easily the most important source of international investment.

Britain's relative industrial decline after 1870

The commanding position of Britain in the world economy for much of the nineteenth century was, however, already being progressively

3. In rough terms, the *balance of trade* shows the payments made and received because of current imports and exports of actual goods (visible trade); the *balance of payments on current account* includes this but also adds the trade in services, like banking, insurance, and shipping (invisible trade); the *balance of payments on capital account* records all other transactions—mainly capital transfers (government and private) and changes in the stocks of gold and foreign exchange.

4. Britain's net foreign earnings on selected items, 1816–1913 (Source: Imlah, *Economic Elements in the Pax Britannica*, Harvard U.P., Table 4, pp. 70–5):

Average of	Merchandise trade £m.	Insurance £m.	Shipping £m.	Profits on foreign trade, etc. £m.	Interest and dividends £m.
1816–20	−8·98	2·96	9·92	5·96	1·74
1866–70	−58·12	13·2	44·5	26·36	30·82
1911–13	−134·30	26·57	100·33	53·10	187·93

eroded well before 1914. To a significant extent Britain's dominant position had arisen because she was the first to become a modern industrial nation. As other countries industrialised, much of this lead was bound to disappear. Indeed, the eventual industrial superiority of the United States—larger, with greater resources, technically mature, and with a skilled and growing population—was always clear to the perceptive: the *Economist*, for example, had in 1851 commented that it was 'as certain as the next eclipse' that the industrial output of the United States would soon surpass that of Britain.

Thus there was nothing especially disturbing about the relative decline in Britain's economic position that was discernible from about 1870 onwards. It was inconceivable, for example, that Britain could have continued to produce—as she did in 1870—more pig-iron than the rest of the world put together. None the less the pace and extent of Britain's relative decline were, in some respects, disquieting. By 1913, for example, the United States production of pig-iron was already three times as great as that of Britain, while that of Germany was also about 50 per cent above British output. Britain's share of total world manufacturing production fell from about one-third in 1870 to about one-seventh in 1913.

Perhaps of still more significance, however, is the possibility that by 1913 the country was lagging in initiative and enterprise, the qualities which were widely thought to have produced its nineteenth-century pre-eminence. Two main trends may be adduced to support a belief in Britain's dwindling competitiveness. Firstly, the rate of growth of the economy appears to have shifted perceptibly downwards somewhere around the 1890s,[5] which hastened the speed at which thrusting rivals threatened—in economic terms—to overhaul Britain. In addition, there was mounting evidence that Britain was failing to develop the newer industries, such as electrical engineering, some branches of the chemical industry, and motor vehicle manufacture.

The possible causes of Britain's supposed decline in enterprise are numerous and hotly disputed. They include a belief that Britain

5. The annual percentage rate of growth of real gross domestic product in the U.K. (Source: R. C. O. Matthews, 'Some Aspects of Post-war Growth in the British Economy', *Trans. of Manchester Statistical Society*, 1964):

1856–1899	2·0
1899–1913	1·1
1924–1937	2·3
1948–1962	2·5

lagged behind other countries in the provision of technical education; that businessmen had become less eager and energetic; that investment was discouraged by low wages and a plentiful supply of labour; and that too much of the country's capital was being invested abroad. Without entering into the debate, it can at least be said that one major result was that the structure of British industry was relatively slow to change in the years before 1914. The basic resources of labour, capital, land, and enterprise remained heavily committed to such industries as textiles and coal. There had been little shift of resources into the pace-setting industries of the twentieth century. This inappropriate industrial balance was to constitute a major problem of the inter-war years.

Overseas trade and finance, 1870–1914

In other areas Britain's retreat from its mid-Victorian supremacy was less marked. In international trade it was natural that, with the emergence of strong industrial competitors, Britain's share of total world trade would fall. There were, however, important compensating features. World trade as a whole during this period was growing quite strongly, and this helped to cushion the impact of increasing competition on Britain's trading position. The volume of British exports grew by about $2\frac{1}{2}$ per cent a year from 1873 to 1898, and then by about double that rate until 1914. And although her share of world trade dropped from 23 per cent to 17 per cent between 1870 and 1913, Britain was still the world's leading trading nation.

In trading terms, then, it could be argued that Britain's position of primacy indicated a continuing strength. But—even before 1914—increasing notice was being taken of several aspects of this trade which carried a chill message for the future. Thus the proportion of Britain's exports which were going to countries and territories within the British Empire rose from 25 per cent in 1870 to 40 per cent in 1913, a change which was widely regarded as an indicator of Britain's failure to withstand foreign competition in general world markets.

Similarly, it was disquieting that exports were dominated by a comparatively narrow range of long-established products—textiles, coal, ships, iron, and steel. The rate of growth of future world demand for these products was likely to slow down, while the most important of them—cotton textiles—was usually the first industry to be established in newly-industrialising countries. In addition, more and more countries had from 1870 onwards adopted measures to protect their home industries, making it more difficult to sell them British manufactures. All these constituted substantial long-term problems for British trade, problems which—in hindsight at least—had already clearly emerged before 1914. They were problems, too, with major implications for the home economy, where the level of activity and employment was closely affected by the export sector. They were problems which cast their shadows—greatly deepened by the disruptions of war—across the years after 1919.

Before 1914 the potential seriousness of Britain's declining competitiveness was partly disguised by her very strong position in international finance. Britain was the major source of capital for investment overseas and London was undoubtedly the world's dominant financial centre. Between 1870 and 1914 British capital assets overseas increased more than five-fold from around £700 million to nearly £4,000 million. The amounts invested abroad were particularly large in the decade or so before the First World War—indeed, immediately before 1914 nearly 10 per cent of the total national income was being invested in other countries.

The desirability of this form of investment is often questioned. It is argued, for example, that the capital which flowed overseas meant that there was a relative lack of funds for investment in Britain, and that this partly accounts for the inadequate development of the newer industries. This is debatable. Much more certain are two broad effects of this foreign investment on Britain's overseas trading position. In the first place, the mounting income which was received in interest and dividend payments on foreign capital ensured that the current balance of payments was persistently favourable. Secondly, these flows of British capital undoubtedly stimulated demand for British exports. Thus any failure to continue the flow was bound to undermine a major source of the apparent stability and security of Britain's pre-1914 position.

Summary

In general, then, Britain had largely dominated the world economy until about 1870: thereafter, although her output and trade still continued to expand, she lost ground relative to other countries. And although this was substantially a natural and unavoidable development, there were indications that the comparative decline was—even before 1914—proceeding further and faster than was comfortable. The First World War greatly aggravated the unfavourable trends and also eroded some of the strength of Britain's international financial position. By 1919, therefore, the British economy was faced with problems which could not prudently be postponed; but the economic legacy was better described as vaguely disquieting rather than alarming.

The general pattern of the book

It is against this background that the present book will indicate the broad development of the economy in the half century or so after the First World War. In a slim volume there is no possibility of satisfying all the expectations that might arise from the title of *Britain and the World Economy, 1919–1970*, and so the emphasis is placed firmly on tracing the economic development of Britain during these years. The international economy is in general treated only in so far as it affects and influences the British economy. Even on so restrictive a basis, however, external influences obtrude quite frequently. Foreign trade was, and is, an important part of Britain's total economic activity.[6]

Changes in the international economy always have, therefore, an underlying significance for economic development in Britain. None the less the extent of this significance varies from time to time. An attempt is made in the pages which follow to reflect something of this variation. Thus, for example, there was in the 1920s a general desire to re-create the international economy as nearly as possible along the lines of its pre-1914 image. For this reason, and also because Britain had played a central part in the pre-1914 mechanism for conducting world trade, it was natural that international economic affairs loomed large in Britain during this decade. The first two chapters of the book, dealing with Britain in the 1920s, thus give much prominence to these broad international considerations.

The attempts of the 1920s to run world trade along pre-war lines ended in failure and disaster. Between 1929 and 1933 there was a general breakdown in the international trading and financial mechanism. Britain with its heavy involvement in world trade was naturally greatly affected by these events. Chapter 3, which deals with these years, is thus largely dominated by an account of these general international trends and their effects on the British economy.

6. Thus, for example, the value of U.K. imports as a percentage of gross national product was, in 1913, 30·4 per cent; in 1930, 22·8 per cent, and in 1969, 21·1 per cent. The comparable figures for U.K. exports are 20·8 per cent, 12·5 per cent, and 19·0 per cent.

The story of the 1930s is quite different. The general shock and disillusionment induced by the collapse of the international economy led countries almost everywhere to look inwards upon themselves. There was a growth of nationalism and autarchy as countries attempted to insulate themselves from what the Great Crash of 1929–33 had made to appear as the disrupting fluctuations of international trade. There were sharp limits to the extent to which Britain could indulge in such flights of economic self-sufficiency, and she was therefore soon attempting to mend some international fences. But, even for Britain, economic policy was concerned mainly with domestic affairs, and for this reason Chapter 4 contains only passing references to the international economy.

The opportunity is also taken in that chapter to examine some important economic characteristics which prevailed throughout the inter-war years. These include, for example, the great regional variation in the incidence of unemployment, with much higher levels of unemployment in Scotland and Wales, the north-east and Lancashire, than in the Midlands and south-east; the related trends concerning the growth of newer industries; and the relative decline of some of the older-established industries.

The position after 1945 is rather more complicated. These years have seen an extensive revival of international economic co-operation and the creation of a number of new international institutions. Britain has played its part in this process, and the home economy has undoubtedly gained from the resulting healthier state of world trade. All this, though briefly treated, is not however the central concern of the last two chapters. In the judgment of the author—many would disagree—the crucial interaction between Britain and the world economy was (from Britain's point of view) the way in which internal developments in Britain were repeatedly constrained by balance of payments difficulties. The emphasis in Chapters 5 and 6, therefore, is very much on the way the British economy and British economic policy reacted and adjusted to this external constraint. Thus developments in Europe (such as the European Payments Union of the 1950s and the establishment of the Common Market, and of the European Free Trade Association) are given rather scant treatment.

There is, then, substantial variation and much selectivity in the way in which the international economy is treated. The emphasis is upon the economic development of Britain. Even here, however, the coverage is far from comprehensive. Industrial relations, for example, receive only sporadic attention—in the early 1920s and the

1960s—at points where they seem to have had a more or less direct bearing on the growth of the economy as a whole. No attempt is made to present a continuous account of the development of industrial relations in Britain in these years, and still less attention is directed towards the labour movement generally. These exclusions convey no judgments on the intrinsic importance of these issues: they do indicate a judgment about their significance for the very broad story of Britain's economic growth presented in this volume. Similarly, and for the same kind of reason, comparatively little attention is given to the organisation of British industry—the size of firms, the degree to which ownership was concentrated, and the prevalence of restrictive practices.

Chapter 1

The 1920s: the Course of Economic Development

The major problems

The British economy during the inter-war years was faced with two overriding problems. The first was the need to re-allocate its economic resources away from those industries which were declining, or growing only slowly, and towards those industries which were expanding most rapidly. This was a particularly formidable problem because the declining industries—such as coal-mining, cotton, and ship-building—were Britain's old staple industries, industries in which an exceptionally large proportion of her capital and labour was employed.

The second major problem was the need to restore the steady expansion of world trade which had been disrupted by the First World War, and which had been so prominent a feature of the international economy before 1913. This was clearly a vital prerequisite for the economic well-being of a major trading nation like Britain. The two problems were, moreover, closely linked, because before 1913 the staple industries were responsible for most of Britain's export trade.

The industrial structure

During the 1920s relatively little progress was made towards the solution of the first of these problems, the alteration in Britain's industrial structure. This was partly because the war and the immediate post-war boom greatly stimulated activity in many of the staple industries and falsely encouraged the belief that they faced an expansionary future. Even after these industries entered upon a long period of depression after 1921, a depression which—because of their size—coloured the entire economy, the awareness only slowly emerged that the problem was a permanent one. It was thought that they would revive once world trade recovered. The nature of the difficulty only began to be realised when the export sectors of the British economy failed to share appreciably in the brief buoyancy which was experienced in world trade between 1925 and 1929. For this reason the main consideration of the structural problems of the economy is postponed till Chapter 4, which deals with the 1930s, although some indication of the importance of these problems in explaining the economic development of the 1920s is included in Chapter 2.

The international economy

During the 1920s it was the second problem, that of reviving the international economy, which received most attention. Towards this end, Britain participated in many—and initiated several—international conferences during these years.[1] In particular, the World Economic Conference held in May 1927 roundly declared that 'the time has come to put an end to the increase in tariffs and to move in the opposite direction'.[2] The removal or reduction of tariff barriers to trade was an important part of the general efforts to stimulate the international economy, and it was one in which Britain, as a major exporting nation, had a vital interest. At the time, however, Britain's own tariff levels were still very low since, with some minor modifications, Britain still adhered to the policy of free trade which she had adopted in the middle of the nineteenth century.

A much more specific British contribution to the restoration of world trade was contained in the policy of returning to the gold standard. The gold standard mechanism was the basis of the pre-1913 system of international trade, and Britain (notably the City of London) had been central to the working of that mechanism. Britain was both a major trading nation—although even before 1913 her relative importance in world trade had been declining—and the major source of international capital. If this trading mechanism was to be restored—and there was a general belief that the system had contributed substantially to the economic progress of the world before 1914—an obvious prerequisite was that Britain herself should return to the gold standard. The economic history of Britain in the 1920s is greatly coloured by the preoccupation with this policy and with its effects. This is, indeed, the central theme of the present

1. League of Nations, *Commercial Policy in the Inter-war Period*, Geneva, 1942.

2. *Ibid.*, p. 39. The declaration had, however, only very limited effects and even these were only temporary. From the beginning of the world economic crisis in 1929 there was a general movement towards higher tariffs, a movement in which Britain eventually participated.

chapter, and this demands that a short explanation of the main features of the gold standard system should be given in a brief, simplified, and rather formal fashion.

The mechanism of the gold standard

An international economic system requires some means of making balance of payments adjustments. At any given time some countries will be running trade deficits (in the simplest sense this may be taken to mean that the value of the goods and services which they are importing exceeds the value of their exports)[3] and other countries will be running trade surpluses. As long as these discrepancies are merely temporary—arising, perhaps, from seasonal shifts in demand —they can be met out of a country's reserves of gold or foreign exchange. If, however, the imbalances are more permanent, some means must exist for their correction.

In broad terms, there are three ways in which adjustments can be effected—by changes in exchange rates, by changes in prices, and by changes in income.[4] In each case the effect is achieved by reducing in one way or another the deficit country's demand for imports and increasing the foreign demand for its exports.

Adjustment through exchange-rate changes can be incorporated in a number of ways, varying from freely-fluctuating exchange rates to a once-and-for-all devaluation. The process operates by making the currency of a deficit country worth less in terms of other currencies. Thus the imports of the deficit country become dearer while its exports, in terms of foreign currency, become cheaper. Imports tend to fall and exports to rise and hence the balance of payment disequilibrium tends to be corrected.

Adjustment through price changes requires that the internal level of prices in the deficit country should be reduced (and, ideally, that internal prices in surplus countries be increased). The effect is to make the exports of the deficit country more competitive and also to make its home products more competitive with imported goods. Again imports are reduced and exports stimulated to produce a tendency towards balance of payments equilibrium.

Adjustment through income changes has only been understood

3. For a more precise treatment see H. Katrak, *International Trade and the Balance of Payments* (Chapters 2 and 4) in this series.

4. This is assuming relatively free market conditions. It is also possible to control deficits by imposing very tight direct controls on trade—exchange controls, import quotas, etc.—but these severely curtail the total level of trade.

comparatively recently, the theoretical elaboration of this process really having been made in the 1940s. The process requires that the deficit country should reduce—perhaps by a policy of deflation—the aggregate level of internal incomes. The reduced income will mean a lower level of demand and this will improve the balance of payments situation in two ways. Firstly, part of the reduction in demand will be a reduction in the demand for imported goods. And secondly, the lower level of internal demand will make producers more eager to sell their goods to foreigners. The trend towards lower imports and increased exports works to adjust the external balance.

Fixed exchange rates

Under the gold standard system, exchange rates between different national currencies were normally regarded as fixed. The value of each currency was normally fixed in terms of gold—this usually meant that the central bank was always ready to buy and sell gold at the given rate, and that there was a fairly direct relationship between a country's gold reserves and its total money supply.

Suppose that Britain's balance of payments with the rest of the world was in deficit. The fixed exchange rate under a gold standard system meant that this could not be corrected by letting the value of sterling fall in relation to other currencies. There was, however, supposed to be an automatic mechanism of adjustment. The British deficit would cause an outflow of gold from Britain, which meant that Britain's money supply was automatically decreased. This was supposed to lead to a fall in British prices which would encourage exports and discourage imports. There was thus an automatic tendency to restore equilibrium.

In addition, these adjustments were facilitated by the use of interest rates. Under the gold standard rules, a country losing gold raised its interest rates. This would, in the short run, attract capital in, and hence raise the demand for, its currency. In the longer run the dearer credit would tend to correct the trade imbalance. The credit contraction would encourage exports and discourage imports either because (as was thought at the time) it would reduce the price level in the deficit country, or because it reduced incomes there.

Adjustment through price and income changes

Both before 1914 and during the 1920s, the contemporary explanations of the working of the gold standard laid stress on the part played by price changes in securing external adjustment. In practice, however, most of the adjustment was probably secured through income movements. Even in a non-inflationary age it was not easy to reduce the level of prices quickly. There were many institutional rigidities. In particular, price reductions usually entailed some reduction in costs, and this required a reduction in wages which trade unions were likely to resist.

As we shall see, these restraints were particularly important in the 1920s. On the other hand a general policy of deflation, a restriction of credit, and a raising of interest rates tended to discourage investment, which led to lower incomes, a reduced level of demand, and higher unemployment. Indeed, it was the realisation that adjustments under the gold standard required reductions in the levels of internal incomes and employment that eventually came to make the system seem an unattractive basis for an international economy. And it was the experience of the inter-war years that was largely responsible for this realisation.

Strictly, the process of adjustment should always have been accelerated by the authorities in the creditor country taking the opposite course—that is, taking the inflow of gold as a signal to raise the level of prices and income. But although the rule was for deficit countries to contract credit and creditor countries to expand credit, its operation tended to be asymmetrical: there was not as much pressure on creditors to conform as there was on debtors.

The whole system, of course, required the central bank to make its major objective the maintenance of the convertibility of the currency at the fixed rate. Internal monetary and fiscal policy had to be geared to external changes. This restraint applies to some degree to any system of maintaining fixed exchange rates.

The 1920s: a summary of the course of economic change

The 1920s was a decade of economic trouble and disillusion. The troubles can be inferred from a brief chronicle of economic events.

After a short post-armistice pause, the economy was—from about about March 1919 until the middle of 1920—increasingly active. The basis of this rather frantic boom was the need, both at home and abroad, to re-stock after the war. The boom cracked in the summer of 1920 and the fall in activity continued until 1922. The cyclical nature of this swing from boom to slump had been a long-established characteristic of economic activity in industrial societies and so, up to this stage, the only exceptional feature was the unusual steepness of both the boom of 1919–20 and of the slump of 1920–22.

Revival began at the end of 1922, but it was unusually slow and incomplete. A peak of sorts (unemployment was still 10 per cent) was reached in 1929, but the progress towards this had been very halting. This was partly because of the effects of industrial strife: the brief general strike and the lengthy coal strike of 1926, for example, greatly reduced industrial output in that year. A more enduring cause was the relative stagnation of exports. There was thus a protracted period of distress in such basic export industries as textiles, shipbuilding, and coal-mining. From these industries derived most of the heavy unemployment which, as we shall see, was another marked characteristic of the British economy in the 1920s and contributed significantly to the economic troubles of the decade.

The disillusionment with the performance of the economy in this decade stemmed from two major sources. In the first place, the contrast between the economic achievement and the hopes which had been engendered during and after the war was especially marked. Some of the men who had fought to build 'a land fit for heroes' found themselves transferred, with only a short respite, from lines of soldiers to the lines of the army of the unemployed, and became bitter and cynical.

The second major source of disillusionment did not arise until after 1925, when world trade did strongly revive. Britain shared very inadequately in the general international boom which followed. Until that time the disappointing performance of the British economy could be attributed to a temporary failure of world trade: thereafter the difficulties had to be regarded as more fundamental.

The post-war boom, 1919–20

The winter that followed the ending of the war in November 1918 was one of considerable difficulty and dislocation. In some degree this was almost unavoidable. By 1918 the economy was, to all intents and purposes, on a full war footing: resources were, with varying degrees of efficiency, directed towards war purposes and were not allocated in response to market changes. The redirection of resources towards peacetime needs was bound to lead to considerable disruption, particularly as many war orders were cancelled more abruptly than factories could adjust their production schedules. These problems were, moreover, compounded by the frightening ravages of a serious epidemic of influenza; by serious shortages of many of the resources needed for adjustment (coal, for example, was acutely scarce during the first winter of peace); and by the troops' impatient rejection of the plans which had been laid for their orderly demobilisation.

None the less, the most striking feature of the immediate transition from a wartime to a peacetime economy was not that dislocation had occurred, but that it was so brief and so mild. By March 1919 it was already clear that a strong economic recovery was under way.

This was fed by a number of powerful circumstances. Indeed, in hindsight, these factors seem self-evident and make the contemporary fears of immediate large-scale depression and unemployment seem highly unreal. There was, for example, an enormous demand from overseas for the British exports which had been substantially curtailed during the war. At the same time there was a strong home demand—the money for which derived from the high levels of wartime employment and the soldiers' demobilisation pay—for the numerous consumer goods which had been kept in short supply by the needs of war.

Even so the boom of 1919–20 could hardly have developed without the operation of other factors. In particular, uncertainty about two of these—whether the vast army of soldiers could be absorbed into the labour force and whether credit would be available for industrial investment—gave substance to the fears of heavy unemployment. In the event, the task of absorbing the demobilised soldiers and redundant munition workers was partially eased by the, apparently voluntary, withdrawal from the labour market of about three-quarters of a million women workers. Of still greater significance was the government's policy of easy credit facilities. This was by no means a foregone conclusion. It involved a specific rejection of any intention to make a rapid return to the gold standard.[5] Throughout

5. The wartime coalition government with David Lloyd George as prime minister was overwhelmingly returned by a general election held in December 1918, immediately after the Armistice. This government held office until October 1922 when the Conservative majority broke away from the coalition. There followed two Conservative governments, first under Bonar Law (October 1922 to May 1923) and then under Stanley Baldwin until January 1924. From January to November 1924 the first Labour Government under Ramsey MacDonald held office, though it depended on Liberal support since it did not have an overall majority in the House of Commons. A Conservative government under Stanley Baldwin then held office from the end of 1924 to June 1929, when it was replaced by the second Labour Government.

the war years Britain remained formally—though not *de facto*—on the gold standard. It was not until March 1919 that the formal adherence to gold was abandoned. A major consideration in this decision was the realisation that any rapid return to gold at the pre-war parity would require—since British prices had doubled during the war years—a policy of sharp deflation. For a government already afraid of unemployment such a policy was highly unattractive; and its rejection meant that the boom which, by March 1919, was gathering force under the pressure of demand was not hindered by financial stringency.

The upsurge of activity was sharp but brief. The pressure of demand was at first the dominant feature. It outran both the adjustment and the increase in output and so spilled over into rising prices. The pace of the rise in prices was indeed faster in the year before March 1920 than it had been for most of the war. Wage rates, though altering neither as much nor as fast as prices, were also pushed upwards. By April 1920 the economy was virtually at a full employment level.

It was also about to turn downwards, although the signs of this were not very evident for a further three months. Some part of this downswing was probably inevitable. The pent-up post-war demand was bound to moderate with time and hence to lessen the pressure that was pushing up prices. This removed much of the basis for the feverish demand for capital investment, which had been a marked feature of the boom. The actual course of the downturn was, however, greatly increased by government policy. A sharp deflationary pressure was applied to an economy which was in any case declining in activity.

The return to the gold standard in 1925

The exertion of deflationary pressure by the government at a time when activity within the economy was falling looks, to modern eyes, as if the government had mistimed its management of the economy. But government policy in the early 1920s was not primarily concerned with attempting to sustain the level of activity in the economy: it was concerned mainly with moving towards a restoration of the gold standard. Indeed, one of the attractions of the gold standard was that it largely avoided the need for the government to manage the economy at all.

The Cunliffe Committee

The policy of restoration sprang directly from the findings of the Cunliffe Committee on Currency and Foreign Exchanges.[6] It is, indeed, not too fanciful to say that the findings of this enquiry largely shaped internal economic policies and trends for at least the first half of the 1920s. It was able to do so not because it possessed any exceptional authority—its two brief reports were, indeed, extraordinarily lacking in any serious discussion of the issues involved—but because its view coincided with those of most of the politicians, financiers, businessmen, economists, and all those who wished to see the pre-war *status quo* restored, and these represented the most influential, though not necessarily the most numerous, section of the country. The major finding in its interim report was expressed with confident and uncompromising directness: 'In our opinion it is imperative that after the war the conditions necessary to the maintenance of an effective gold standard should be restored without delay.'

There is little in this interim report to suggest that the Committee realised the magnitude of the task they were recommending. During the war the normal conduct of trade had been considerably disrupted. In particular, the war had seen the severance of the monetary links between countries. Before 1914 each country that was on the gold standard—and this meant most countries of any significance in international trade—fixed the value of its currency in terms of gold and was committed to maintain this relationship. The common link with gold meant that there was a fixed rate of exchange between different currencies, and this normal stability facilitated trade by substantially removing the risks of currency fluctuations.

Fixed exchange rates can, however, be maintained only so long as the prices in different countries remain more or less in line with each other. This was impossible during the war, when the value of the currencies of most countries depreciated but not at a uniform rate, so that the pre-1914 relative values between currencies were no longer appropriate. These discrepancies, moreover, became even more marked in the immediate post-war years, expecially as, between

6. In January 1918 the Treasury and the Minister for Reconstruction appointed a Committee under Lord Cunliffe, Governor of the Bank of England, to consider the currency problems which would arise in the post-war period and the steps which should be taken to restore normal conditions. It issued two reports: an interim report in August 1918 and a very brief final report in December 1919.

1921 and 1923, the currency in several important countries of central Europe—Germany, Austria, and Hungary—became worthless because it was printed and issued in ever-increasing quantities. Uncertainty about what was going to happen to currencies was thus a significant barrier to the growth of world trade.

The problems involved in a return to the gold standard were also increased for Britain in the immediate post-war years. The Committee's interim report had been submitted in August 1918, before the end of the war. The general fears that the armistice would bring economic dislocation had thus made it seem prudent to postpone the implementation of the report. However, the unanticipated boom of 1919 not only largely dispelled the gloomy forebodings about the process of transition to peace but also, by its intensity, raised a quite different set of fears. There was much anxiety, especially in the City, because the powerful inflationary pressure seemed to be carrying the country away from a 'sound' currency at a faster pace than had happened during the war. Thus the final report of the Cunliffe Committee, issued in the boom condition of December 1919, received an especially warm welcome from all those who feared that conditions were getting out of hand. The Committee reiterated its earlier proposals and called for immediate action: 'Increased production, cessation of government borrowings and decreased expenditure both by the Government and by each individual member of the nation are the first essentials to recovery. These must be associated with the restoration of the pre-war methods of controlling the currency and credit system for the purpose of re-establishing at an early date a free market for gold in London.'

The movement back to the gold standard

The government began the serious pursuit of these conditions—necessary for the restoration of the gold standard—with the budget of April 1920. The chase was to prove long and painful, but it got away to a brisk start. This was partly because the downward trend was world-wide: falling prices and declining activity in other countries meant lower prices in Britain and a reduced demand for British exports. In particular, the decline in world prices of food and raw materials meant that wholesale prices fell very rapidly during the first year,[7] while unemployment in the United Kingdom rose dramati-

7. *The Economist* index (1913 = 100) stood at 306 in April 1920, and 183 in April 1921.

cally from less than 3 per cent to nearly 20 per cent. Retail prices and wage rates lagged behind, continuing to rise until the end of 1920 and not falling rapidly until nearly the middle of 1921.

All these indices tended to level out about the middle of 1922. There was some increase in the level of activity between 1922 and 1924, especially noticeable in the drop in unemployment and in the rise in industrial production.[8] Conditions then worsened again until 1926.

There were two significant features of the fluctuations in the level of economic activity during the first half of the 1920s. The first was that, once the brief boom had broken in 1920, these fluctuations took place around a level of unemployment which was exceptionally high. None the less—and this was the second important characteristic—although there was a very sharp fall in the level of prices and wages, British prices were still high relative to those of some other countries. It did not much matter that British prices—even after the sharp deflation—were higher than they had been before 1914, since all countries had experienced inflationary pressures. It did matter that the persisting degree of inflation seemed to be higher in Britain than in some other countries, and especially in comparison with the United States.

The essential prerequisite for a return to the gold standard at the pre-war parity was that British prices should be brought back into line with those of her major competitors. In so far as the exchange rate between the pound and the dollar indicated the relative price levels in Britain and the United States, this position was never quite achieved. The pre-war parity had been $4·86 to the £. The rate had fallen by early 1920 to $3·40, but thereafter it rose to $4·70 at the beginning of 1923, only to fall away again to about $4·40.

The fall persisted until after the middle of 1924, when the authorities adopted a deliberate policy of pushing up the exchange rate by raising Bank Rate to attract foreign funds. By April 1925 the rate had been driven up close to the pre-war parity. Winston Churchill, as Chancellor, announced Britain's return to the gold standard at that parity in his budget speech of 28 April. Thus, so long as this was adhered to, Britain was unable to correct any imbalance in her external position by lowering the parity—that is, by reducing the value of the pound in relation to other currencies. Especially in the

8. The average monthly numbers registered as unemployed fell from 1·5 million in 1922 to 1·1 million in 1924. The index of industrial production rose from 95 in 1922 to 100 in 1924. B. R. Mitchell and P. Deane, *Abstract of British Historical Statistics*, 1962, pp. 66, 272.

absence of any 'substantial degree of protection the only alternative, if British exports were uncompetitive, would be to lower the level of domestic costs.

British exports were in fact uncompetitive in price, but it proved exceptionally difficult to lower domestic costs. For some two years before the decision was taken to return to gold at the old parity, a situation had developed in which the level of British costs—especially in the export industries—was too high relative to those of overseas competitors; and yet the already very high levels of unemployment—especially in the export industries—made it very difficult for the government to depress these costs further by increasing its deflationary pressure.

There was, however, some hope that the gap would be filled from the other direction: that foreign—and especially United States—prices would rise.[9] On the surface there seemed to be quite good grounds for expecting American prices to rise. This was because, like Britain, the United States had experienced a wild, brief post-war boom and a subsequent sharp depression. Unlike Britain, this had been followed by a period of obviously rising activity and, as this continued, there seemed good reason to expect American prices and costs to rise. For a number of complex reasons, however, one of the peculiar features about the economic upsurge in America during the 1920s was the comparative stability of wages and prices: the British equation was not to be balanced from outside. Thus it seemed that a return to gold at the old parity would imply further cuts in wages in, especially, the export sectors of British industry.

It might seem that the obvious course was not to return at the old parity: this would apparently avoid the need to cut costs. It has been suggested that this was not an option that was open to British policymakers. For, even if Britain had adopted a lower dollar parity, other countries returning to gold later would simply have fixed their parities lower still.[10] In particular France (and Belgium) quite

9. The discussion over foreign price trends centred in fact almost entirely on prices in the United States. There were two main reasons for attaching particular importance to the level of U.S. prices. Firstly, the United States was a significant market for British exports—taking about 10 per cent of total exports in the mid-1920s. Secondly, and much more crucial, the United States had become extremely important relative to world trade as a whole and in the 1920s had taken over Britain's pre-1913 role of being easily the largest international lender.

10. R. S. Sayers, 'The Return to Gold, 1925', in L. S. Pressnell (ed.), *Studies in the Industrial Revolution*, 1958, p. 321. See also S. Pollard (ed.), *The Gold Standard and Employment Policies*, 1970.

deliberately under-valued their parities in relation to sterling when they returned to gold in 1926.[11]

There is some substance in this view but it seems probable that the removal of the over-valuation of sterling in relation to the dollar would have relieved some of the pressure on the British economy, even though the franc might have been still more under-valued in relation to the dollar. It would certainly have provided some relief from the pressures of Germany's resurgence in the world export markets from 1925 onwards. Such considerations are, however, largely irrelevant, since the idea of fixing a lower parity was given little serious consideration at the time. There was an overwhelming presumption that the old parity would be adopted, that not to do so would constitute a default by Britain and would jeopardise London's status as an international monetary centre.

The wisdom of returning to gold at the old parity may be debatable. What is clear is that, once the decision had been taken, the need to maintain this parity was an important influence affecting the trend of economic events in Britain for the rest of the decade— just as the determination to return to gold had been an important factor influencing the level of economic activity in the first half of the decade. However, the level of costs in the export sector was not, in the event, significantly reduced and this made it necessary to maintain interest rates at a level which was—given the heavy unemployment—quite high. This was because, in the absence of a favourable trading position, it was necessary to attract short-term funds into Britain, especially as long-term investment overseas was continued. Apart from two brief months at 4 per cent in 1925, Bank Rate was fixed at either $4\frac{1}{2}$ or 5 per cent until 1929, when it was moved still further upwards. Partly as a result of this, prices continued to drift downwards, producing an atmosphere that was relatively unfavourable to rapid development. In addition, because the external situation required higher interest rates, the development of new industries was to some degree impeded by the consequent discouragement of investment.

The gold standard and industrial relations, 1919–26

One of the fields which was inevitably much affected by the general climate of the 1920s was that of industrial relations. The labour

11. The stabilisation of the French franc in December 1926 was only on a *de facto* basis, but the same rate was adopted when the official return to the gold standard was made in June 1928.

movement had emerged from the war with a greatly enhanced sense
of assurance. On the industrial front the anxiety of the government
to secure the full co-operation of the unions during the war had led
to many concessions, and these successes had contributed to a
doubling of trade union membership. On the political front the
Labour Party became better organised—a new constitution was
adopted in February 1918—and emerged from the election of December 1918 as the official Opposition with 59 members. Enthusiasm
and optimism abounded, partly engendered by the psychological
boost of the Russian revolution.

Labour relations in a rising market

At the beginning of 1919 it seemed probable that the labour
movement would secure substantial concessions on both the industrial and the political fronts. The general expectation of the time—
though some viewed the prospect with elation and others with gloom
—was that several of the key industries would certainly be nationalised. Moreover, the position of labour seemed to be very strong: the
initial, and well-grounded, fears of acute industrial unrest made the
government anxious to placate the workers. And when these fears
largely disappeared in the brief boom, the high level of activity
placed the trade unions in a powerful bargaining position.

The miners attempted to exploit this situation early in 1919 by
presenting sweeping demands for a six-hour day, dramatic wage
increases, and the nationalisation of the industry, demands which
were supported by an overwhelming vote for strike action. Action
was postponed, however, on an offer of an investigating commission
—the Sankey Commission—and government promises to accept its
findings. An interim report appeared on 20 March and a second
report on 20 June:[12] on each occasion the members were divided
in their proposals and this enabled the government to become increasingly evasive. The miners secured part of their bread-and-butter
demands—a seven-hour day and an increase of wages of 2 shillings
(10 new pence) a day—but the government eventually rejected the
proposals to nationalise the mines, and even neglected to implement
a firm commitment to nationalise mining royalties, which had been
one of the few unanimous proposals of the Commission.

This was a crucial episode in several ways. It left the miners with a,
highly understandable, feeling that they had been betrayed by

12. In March there were, in fact, three separate reports; in June there were four.

relying on government promises, and this was an important factor in determining their views and attitudes in the years ahead. But it also blunted the political demands involved in industrial action: where the miners had failed, no other proposals for nationalisation were likely to succeed. There was still a great deal of industrial unrest and union activity, but its mood changed. At the beginning of 1919 there was a near-revolutionary atmosphere; but as the year wore on—and particularly after the government had out-manoeuvred the miners and had harshly suppressed a police strike in August—union efforts were more concentrated upon using the boom in activity to extract what they could in the form of better wages and conditions. In this some substantial success was obtained: weekly wage-rates, which were fairly static during the first half of 1919, rose rapidly from then until the beginning of 1921. (The London and Cambridge index of wage rates, with July 1914 = 100, rose from 210 in June 1919 to 277 in January 1921.) This rise—at the least—kept pace with rises in the cost of living, and in many industrial sectors involved an increase in real wages.

Labour relations in a falling market

In 1921 the tide turned decisively. Wages and retail prices, which had continued to drift upwards for a while after most indices had turned down in the summer of 1920, now began to fall as the government's deflationary measures began to bite. As so often in the 1920s, the changes were heralded and dramatised by events in the coal industry; and as so often in this industry the issue became much more than a direct matter of wages.

A wage agreement was due to expire on 31 March 1921. The government—which because of the fall in prices was suddenly faced with losses from its control of the industry—announced late in February that the industry would be de-controlled on 31 March, five months earlier than had been intended. The owners insisted on swingeing wage cuts and on a reversion to district agreements: the miners were determined to press for a national wages board. The strike, which started on 1 April, seemed likely for a time to develop into a general stoppage: the miners called for the assistance of the other two unions in the Triple Alliance, the railwaymen and transport workers.[13] These agreed to strike in sympathy, but then seized upon

13. In 1914, just before the war, the miners, railwaymen, and transport workers —seeking power in unity—resolved to negotiate their future wage agreements in

an unguarded and ambiguous statement by the miners' secretary, Frank Hodges, as a pretext to withdraw from this undertaking at the eleventh hour. This was the so-called Black Friday of the trade union movement. Once the threat of a general strike was removed, the miners, in a highly unfavourable economic climate, were doomed to defeat. And when the miners collapsed on 1 July, the way was open for a general reduction of wages.

Thereafter wages and prices fell with extraordinary rapidity during 1922 when, under the influence of the Geddes Committee, government expenditure was also sharply cut back.[14] The most striking feature of the deflation, however, was the very high level of unemployment and its unprecedented persistence after the slump and into the years beyond. This served as one indicator that British costs were still high relative to those of foreign competitors, especially as the unemployment was heavily concentrated in the export sectors. Thus, once the decision had been made to return to the gold standard at the old parity, there was bound to be some pressure to reduce wages further, especially in the export sector.

Once again, the issue centred on the coal industry. On this occasion the miners carried the other unions with them into the General Strike, which started on 3 May 1926 and lasted for nine days. The government made widespread use of the armed forces to provide essential supplies; but despite this, and despite the assistance of very many volunteers—especially students—the stoppage was generally effective. None the less, and despite the highly provocative stance taken by the government, the General Council of the T.U.C. recoiled at the largely unintended revolutionary implications of the strike and unconditionally called a halt—surrendered—on 12 May.

The strike had involved sporadic violence, but no loss of life; its settlement involved widespread victimisation and much bitterness

---

association with each other. This association became known as the Triple Alliance but it proved very difficult to secure any joint action: in particular the threat of a joint strike was usually more formidable than the the reality.

14. The Geddes Committee was appointed in August 1921 to examine the provisional estimates of government expenditure in the following year and to recommend economies. Its chairman was the autocratic Sir Eric Geddes, who had been Minister of Transport in Lloyd George's first post-war government. Its other members were mostly drawn from business. It suggested economies on a scale large enough to embarrass even the government. For the rest of the inter-war period the phrase 'the Geddes axe' became synonymous with calls for cuts in government expenditure: and there was always an articulate body of opinion eager to see this axe wielded.

and loss of dignity. For the miners it was yet another betrayal. Obstinate to the end they struggled on alone for another six months before accepting the inevitable return to longer hours and lower pay. However, apart from the miners and a few other groups—like the railwaymen—there was no general reduction in wages. The reasons for this are not at all clear—the crushing of the miners might have seemed a favourable opportunity to impose reductions, especially as the trade union movement emerged from the general strike weakened in numbers, financial strength, and spirit. But whatever the reasons the result was that British exports remained uncompetitive and the strain of maintaining the gold standard was correspondingly increased.

For much of the decade, then, either the intended, or the actual, return to the gold standard exerted a strong influence on the atmosphere of industrial relations. Perhaps this is what McKenna, the chairman of the Midland Bank and an ex-Chancellor of the Exchequer, implied when he gave Churchill his opinion on the policy of returning to the gold standard: 'There is no escape; you have to go back; but it will be hell.' This policy required reductions in wage rates so extensive that they were bound to lead to widespread clashes; in the event they were never quite pushed through to the extent necessary to bring British prices fully into line with those of, particularly, the U.S.A. The country seemed to reap to the full the bitterness implied in this approach without ever quite grasping the potential rewards.

The gold standard and international trade, 1925–29

An important part of the argument for the restoration of the gold standard had rested on its presumed necessity for the healthy conduct of international trade: the restoration of stability in international currency matters was believed to be an essential prerequisite for the expansion of world trade. The revival of the gold standard was expected to provide this stability and thus to remove, or reduce, the unsettled currency conditions which were clearly disruptive of trade. On this basis it has also been persuasively stated that the return to the gold standard was essentially a policy for raising the level of employment in Britain. 'Britain's unemployment problem was due to depression of world markets; this was partly due to currency disorganisation; therefore get the world's currency instability removed, the former foreign exchange stability restored, and export markets could be expected to revive and Britain's unemployment to dwindle.'[15] One may doubt whether a desire to raise the level of employment formed the main reason for the return to gold. The counsels of the City were much more influential, and so was the simple desire to restore the pre-1914 order of things. It is, however, certainly clear that Britain—as a major trading nation—had both a strong interest in encouraging world trade and a significant influence on international economic policies. Thus the most important single move towards greater international currency stability that was possible in the mid-1920s was for Britain to fix its currency by returning to gold. This, as we have seen, was done in 1925. Did it have the anticipated effects on trade?

At the general level it does seem to have been effective. The index of the total volume of world trade (1913 = 100) averaged only 82 for the years 1921–25, but leapt to 110 for the average of the years 1926–30. The stabilisation of the major currencies during these years must have made an important contribution to this result. But at the more particular level of British trade the evidence is much less re-assuring. In volume terms, the rise of British trade was conspicuously less striking: imports (1913 = 100) rose from 107 in 1925 to 115 in 1929, exports from 75 to 81. In value terms there was an actual decline between 1925 and 1929 in both imports and exports, the value of imports in 1929 being 92 per cent, and the value of exports 94 per cent, of their 1925 level. Thus in the only inter-war years that were really favourable for trade—the only period in which world trade was rising more rapidly than world production—the value of British trade was falling.

Britain, as a major trading nation, must have benefited from the general increase in trade, but this was presumably more than cancelled out by adverse factors. One of these undoubtedly was the fact that the over-valued pound tended to make British prices higher than those of such foreign competitors as the United States, Germany, and France. In its results, though not in its intentions, the return to the gold standard seems to have been a substantially disinterested action on the part of Britain. It seems to have aided the general level of world trade without directly improving the British trading position.

15. Sayers, *The Return to Gold*, pp. 317–18.

Chapter 2

The 1920s: Sources of Economic Development

At the close of the 1920s and the beginning of the next decade, it became increasingly obvious that the British economy was being dragged down by the general decline in world economic activity. This was made all the more disappointing because Britain seemed to have shared inadequately in the general prosperity that most other countries experienced for at least the second half of the decade.

In the United States the upward trend from the end of 1922 became so prolonged that it encouraged delusions that the economy had solved the problem of the trade cycle, delusions that found expression in the description of the 1920s as 'The New Era' or as the years of 'boundless blue horizons'. In France the internal economic expansion seemed to be solidly based on an extremely under-valued franc, while even the German economy enjoyed a marked, but brittle, activity during the second half of the 1920s. But for Britain the 1920s had opened with an unstable boom which proceeded in an atmosphere of war-generated social unrest and unease. They had continued with a sharply disruptive deflation and downturn; and this had given way to a revival so mild as to have few obvious signs—certainly prices remained stagnant and the fall in the level of unemployment was barely perceptible. All this was in sharp contrast to the optimism which had reigned at the end of the war. Why, after beginning on such high hopes, had the economic performance of the decade been so relatively dismal?

Partly, no doubt, the depth of the disappointment was simply the result of the extravagance of the hope. Beyond this psychological reason, however, the most obvious explanations of the economic difficulties of the 1920s seemed likely to be found among the disturbances created by the First World War.

The direct effects of the war

It was wholly natural that contemporaries should see the war as the main source of their ills. Few people in 1914 had had any conception of what was to come. Thus the totality of the conflict was traumatic in its impact while the ever-growing appetite of trench warfare for men, materials, and money both numbed and overwhelmed contemporaries. It was entirely understandable that an experience so vast, so unforeseen, and so horrible should loom large in men's minds as they sought to explain later economic shortcomings.

To place the blame on the war was, moreover, a natural reaction in quite a different sense. All those who had a vested interest in, or a nostalgic attachment to—the two usually went together—the system as it had operated before 1914 were led to stress the disruptive impact of the war itself. In this way it appeared that the post-war problems could be attributed to an event which was largely external to the economic system. Thus it could plausibly be argued that the pre-war organisation of the economy had been perfectly satisfactory; that this system had, however, been distorted by the needs of war; that these distortions were the source of the post-war difficulties; and thus that the solution was to return as quickly as possible to the pre-war economic system. This was a beguiling line of thought for all those who wished to return to the *status quo ante,* and these (as we have seen) included nearly all the most influential and powerful groups in society.

The loss of capital

More specifically, most people, in thinking of the impact of war, had in mind the loss of capital and manpower which the war had entailed. For Britain, however, the actual destruction of capital was not—in proportion to the total stock—very large. It was, moreover, confined almost entirely to one particular type, shipping. Losses were heavy: excluding fishing boats, they amounted to nearly 2,500 vessels aggregating $7\frac{3}{4}$ million tons gross. However, in assessing the significance of this loss of capital for the economy in the post-war decade, three points need to be borne in mind. Firstly, a substantial part of this loss had already been made good during the war itself, although this had meant that British shipyards were unable to build for foreign orders during these years. Secondly, the remaining deficit was made good in the frantic boom of 1919–20; and thirdly, after 1920 merchant ships were noticeably in excess supply, millions of tons of shipping were laid up, and freight rates were depressed. In all these circumstances, the British economy could hardly be said to be suffering from a loss of capital in so far as this took the form of a lack of ships.

A less direct, but perhaps more significant, way in which the war adversely affected capital was by the enforced delay in replacing buildings, machinery, and equipment. Wartime restrictions and shortages meant that the normal maintenance of the capital stock was partially neglected. There had been, however, some gains in the need to improve equipment in steel and engineering—part of which, at least, was useful in peacetime—to meet the demands for armaments, motor vehicles, and aeroplanes. Yet it is tolerably certain that the physical capital of the nation was in a worse condition in 1919 than it had been in 1913. It is equally probable that these shortcomings— with the important exception of housing—had been made good by 1921.

The loss of manpower

It was even more natural to associate post-war troubles with the wartime slaughter. With some ¾ million men killed—nearly one in ten of all males between the ages of 20 and 45—and a still larger number wounded and disabled, there was in every village, every street— almost every house—an awareness of loss. Despite all this, however, the carnage of the First World War perhaps had relatively little impact on the general population trend. The population of Great Britain was about 2 millions higher in 1921 than it had been in 1911. This was a lower rate of growth[1]—indeed, a substantially lower rate —than during the previous decade. On its own this would suggest that the war had a strong impact. Against this, however, it has to be noted that the downward trend in the rate of growth of population

1. Labour force in the United Kingdom, 1881–1938 (Source: R. C. O. Matthews, 'Some Aspects of Post-war Growth in the British Economy'. *Trans. of Manchester Statistical Society*, 1964):

	Annual rate of growth since last date of:		15–64-year-olds as percentage of total population
	Population	Labour force	
1881	1·0	0·8	58·9
1891	0·8	1·0	60·2
1901	0·9	0·9	62·8
1911	0·9	1·0	63·6
1921	0·4	0·5	65·9
1931	0·4	0·6	68·2
1938	0·4	1·3	69·4

had begun to emerge around the 1880s; that the very low rate of population increase continued throughout the inter-war years; and that the decline in population growth was general among advanced industrial nations, even those which—like Sweden—had not been directly involved in the war.

The economic effects of this demographic pattern are difficult to quantify, but were clearly considerable. The declining rate of population growth removed, or at least weakened, one factor which is generally thought of as having been an important stimulant to the level of aggregate demand—and hence of induced investment—in the nineteenth century. But it is equally clear that these population trends were deep-seated and arose, primarily, not from the shock of war but from the operation of long-run social forces. The wartime losses did affect the age and sex distribution of the population, reducing the proportion in the age group 25–35, and decreasing the number of males to females.[2] This certainly had important and continuing social effects but, in economic terms, the 1920s—with an apparently irreducible minimum of 1 million unemployed—were not years in which the economy was short of manpower.

The effects on trade and industry

Two other wartime effects may be briefly mentioned. First, there were the disruptions imposed on the course of foreign trade. The trading pattern had been of necessity, and substantially, altered and reduced as British industry became more and more centred upon production for direct military needs rather than for exports, and as the shortage of shipping became increasingly acute. Many countries which had tended to take goods from Britain found this source of supply cut off or seriously curtailed: they naturally sought out other suppliers or produced these goods for themselves. But while Britain cut down on her exports, imports could not be easily curtailed. The need for food, raw materials and military supplies maintained a strong pressure of demand. Imports were limited mainly by the shipping constraint, which also determined that supplies should be secured largely by the short-haul passage from the United States and Canada, rather than from Asia and Australasia. Even so there was a mounting trade deficit and to finance this there was a substantial sale of dollar securities. The scale of overseas lending was also decimated.

2. In 1911, in the working population age group (15–70) there were 109 women for every 100 men: in 1921 there were 113 women for every 100 men.

By 1919 the British trading position was significantly different from—and worse than—1913, and these changes were to prove more intractable than was realised in the heady optimism of the immediate post-war boom in exports.

Secondly, the needs of war had led to some distortion of the pattern of the industrial structure in the sense that some industries—like shipbuilding and agriculture—had been stimulated to expand to a degree that was fairly clearly in excess of their normal long-run size. The war had many other—often beneficial—implications for industry. Several industries which before the war had seemed to be lagging seriously behind their long-run potential—aircraft, for example, and some branches of the chemical industry—were given a sharp boost; research was fostered; new management methods were adopted; and, in all areas, old and stultifying ideas and attitudes were at least questioned and, occasionally, disturbed. None the less there is little doubt that in terms of its effects on the structure of industry—the balance of the distribution of industrial activity—the war was unfortunate. It gave too much encouragement to sectors of industry in which—and this had in many cases been emerging even before the war—the real problem was the need to move resources out of them.

The war did not, however, create these industrial distortions: it aggravated or quickened trends which existed anyway. Some further reference will be made to these long-run tendencies later in this chapter, but for the moment it need only be noted that the war had the effect of upsetting the balance of the structure of British industry.

This effect was still further exacerbated by the strength of the post-war boom. The immediate and pressing shortages—both at home and overseas—encouraged speculation and investment on a substantial scale. The speculation mainly drove up prices, especially share prices; the investment involved the construction of productive plant and machinery. The level of demand, which for a brief time was tremendously buoyant, thus stimulated an extensive expansion of capacity as well as a considerable sale of capital equipment at highly inflated prices. A substantial part of the demand was, however, simply for re-stocking and disappeared almost as rapidly as it had emerged, leaving the economy to digest a capital stock over-expanded in capacity and over-expressed in value. This process of digestion was, moreover, made all the more difficult because the demand for re-stocking had been partly concentrated on staple products leading to expansion particularly in the basic industries of steel, coal, shipping, and cotton, a development which added significantly to the difficulties of the decline in these industries that was to come.

The impact of government policy

Another possible explanation of the economic developments of these years lies in the impact of government policy. Allusion has already been made to the most important and most prolonged aspect of this —the movement first to return to, and then to maintain, the gold standard system. Its generally baleful effects on the internal economic climate have been suggested and need not be repeated. There were perhaps two other, partially related, features of policy which could be said to have had some significance for the economy: the very rapid dismantling of the system of wartime controls, and the sustained retrenchment of government expenditure.

The removal of wartime controls

During the course of the war an extensive degree of government control over the economy had developed unobtrusively and almost accidentally. It emerged from a series of improvised responses to recurrent crises. At the end of the war the most general ministerial expectation was that the needs of reconstruction would require the maintenance of many controls for some time to come. However, it soon emerged that this ran counter to general opinion—or, at least, to articulate commercial and industrial opinion which, especially in the profit-lush year of 1919, saw government intervention as an irksome restraint. Policy was quickly adjusted to accommodate this viewpoint and the central direction of the economy was rapidly unravelled. The key ministries—of Food, Shipping, and Munitions— were finally wound up on 31 March 1921; but many of their functions had disappeared long before this, as had numerous *ad hoc* boards and commissions. The government largely divested itself of surplus stores and its numerous factories in a fever of activity in 1919, while by the following year rationing and price controls had been abolished.[3] All this was in sharp contrast to British experience after 1945, when the relaxation of government control was conducted with measured caution while in some respects—like the introduction of bread rationing in 1946—controls were actually increased after the war had ended.

Much of the drive behind the hasty abandonment of controls after

3. R. H. Tawney, 'Abolition of Economic Controls, 1918–21', *Economic History Review*, XII, 1943, pp. 1–30.

the First World War was quasi-emotional, a desire to be released from 'interference'. This abandonment was also fairly widespread: the British trend had its parallels in the United States and France. It had, too, a strong intellectual basis, appealing to the importance of relying on the market as the main regulator of the economy. The market economy would, it was argued, ensure that resources were allocated in the most efficient way, bring demand and supply into balance, and determine the pattern of production in response to the free choices of consumers.

There are many qualifications to be made to this view of the competitive market model, both on theoretical and on practical grounds, but these form an insecure basis from which to attack the desire in 1919 to return—so far as was possible—to a competitive economy. Something roughly like it had operated before 1914 with a reasonable smoothness and a tolerable success. Under it, indeed, Britain had led the international economy. It was natural—particularly for the commercial and industrial community—to wish to return to the old and tried system.

Yet the argument for doing so was more plausible than real: it was indeed based on a delusion. This was the mistaken conviction that all that was needed to restore the pre-1914 system was the removal of government restrictions, the belief that the wartime interventions were readily reversible. In one respect, the essence of a market economy, and the reason why it can function so effectively, is that it may be able to respond very quickly to quite small changes. In this way it enables quite large economic changes—since they are normally spread over substantial periods of time—to be absorbed by a series of more-or-less continuous adjustments. At any one time, therefore, there is a reasonable expectation that the various forces in the market will not be very much out of line.

Against this tendency, the main aim of imposing government controls in wartime is precisely to prevent adjustments taking place in accordance with market forces: consumer demand for many goods must be choked off to ensure that resources are devoted to the purposes of war; scarce food supplies cannot be rationed by the purse if morale and the productive efficiency of the labour force is to be maintained; and so on. Thus the inevitable result of a widespread imposition of government controls—and they were very widespread in Britain from 1916 onwards—is that the economy does get quite sharply out of line. And the market system is less well adapted to coping smoothly with such large and basic adjustments. This weak-

ness was, moreover, considerably exaggerated because the abandonment of controls took place in the more-or-less artificial boom
conditions of 1919. The market is always likely to respond sharply to
such pressures. With hindsight it is clear that the boom largely
derived from the operation of short-term factors—particularly the
release of the pent-up wartime demand—but the market response was
partly to base long-term decisions (such as those involving investment)
on this experience. Thus the policy of indiscriminately and rapidly
removing controls and reverting to reliance on market mechanisms
tended in some important respects to increase the economic distortion
it was intended to correct.

Cutting government expenditure

The other aspect of government action, retrenchment, was perhaps
less of a policy than a reflex action. The restrictive and negative
attitudes of Gladstonian finance had long been entrenched and commanded a largely uncritical acceptance at nearly all levels of government, official, and public opinion. During the war these principles
had been substantially abandoned. In so far as the needs of war led
to a voracious demand for government expenditure this was largely
inevitable. But in the method of financing this expenditure—placing
reliance on borrowing rather than taxation—the canons of Gladstonian finance were departed from with an almost extravagant reckless-
ness. With the end of the war there was a strong tendency to revert
to the more sober pre-war practices.

This involved substantial retrenchment which took two related
forms. There was a direct cutting back in the level of government
activity, while at the same time government expenditure was reduced
much more quickly than government revenue.[4] Expenditure fell

4. Government revenue and expenditure, 1914–1930 (Source: Mitchell and
Deane, *British Historical Statistics*, C.U.P., pp. 394–5, 398–9):

Year ending March	Government expenditure £m.	Government revenue £m.	Year ending March	Government expenditure £m.	Government revenue £m.
1914	192·3	198·2	1925	750·8	799·4
1919	2,579·3	889·0	1926	776·1	812·1
1920	1,665·8	1,339·6	1927	782·4	805·7
1921	1,188·1	1,426·0	1928	773·6	842·8
1922	1,070·1	1,124·9	1929	760·5	836·4
1923	812·5	914·0	1930	781·7	815·0
1924	748·8	837·2			

consistently—and usually sharply—from 1919 to 1924, but 1924 was the first year in which government revenue fell below the wartime level. Indeed until 1921 revenue had risen substantially, despite declining expenditure. Even in 1924, while expenditure stood at less than 30 per cent of its 1919 level, revenue still stood at 94 per cent of its 1919 level.

The effects of policy

Both these trends had important effects on the level of economic activity. They both represented substantial withdrawals from the circular flow of income within the economy. The rapid decline in government expenditure meant that the level of aggregate demand was correspondingly reduced. The initial rise and then much gentler fall in revenue compounded this deflationary tendency, since it reduced the level of private demand.

In the initial boom period the effects of these policies were undoubtedly beneficial: their restrictive effects on the level of demand were more than offset by the violent rise in private expenditure. Indeed, the problems of raising output at this time were so formidable that demand already outran supply. This situation would have been even more evident and the price increases still sharper, but for the curtailment of government expenditure and the increase in government revenue at this time. Once the boom collapsed, however, the policy of retrenchment had economic repercussions which were almost wholly unfavourable. The level of aggregate demand turned sharply downwards from around the middle of 1920, dragging down prices, rapidly increasing the amount of unemployment, and producing a severe slump. This situation was undoubtedly considerably worsened by government fiscal policy: during this year government expenditure was reduced by almost £500 million (or nearly 38 per cent) while government revenue rose by £86 million (or 6 per cent). The result was a massive budget surplus of £245 million. This was largely accidental since the economic effects of government fiscal policy were dimly understood. But it was an unfortunate accident that the most markedly deflationary effects of the policy of retrenchment coincided with the year in which the economic indicators were in any case falling most rapidly and when the economy most needed a helping hand from the government.

For the rest of the decade government fiscal policy was much less obtrusive. After 1923 the level of expenditure was more or less stable, and revenue also levelled out at about the same time. Two points may, however, be made about this. First, it was a stability at what was, compared to the wartime years, a relatively low level. It may be thought that the more appropriate comparison would be with the pre-war situation—government revenue and expenditure in the second half of the 1920s ran at about four times the 1913 level, and adjustment for price changes would still leave most of this difference intact. There is much force in this reasoning; but the essential background to government fiscal policy in the 1920s was the persistence of an unemployment figure of about 1 million, and the level of government expenditure was clearly inadequate to remove this.[5]

The second point is that—apart from its level—the normal net effect of budgetary policy was mildly deflationary because there was a budgetary surplus in these years. Taken together, the implication is that fiscal policy probably did little to make matters worse after 1923, but did nothing to make matters better.

In general, then, and particularly in the crucial early years, the policy of retrenchment had—albeit unconsciously—a discouraging impact on the level of economic activity in the 1920s. In many respects, however, its effects were even more unfortunate in the social field. And here the effects were clearly seen to be the result of deliberate and conscious policies. Thus in the summer of 1921—after retrenchment had already proceeded a long way—a widespread agitation, particularly by the City, led as we have already seen to the appointment of the Geddes Committee to seek out further economies in government expenditure.

Early in 1922 the Committee issued three reports suggesting specific and substantial cuts. These proposals—the so-called Geddes axe—ranged over a wide spectrum of government activity. Its largest cuts, perhaps not surprisingly, were suggested for the largest spenders, the military. The proposals also involved erosion on a number of social

5. To point out this inadequacy is not, however, necessarily to be critical of the governments of the time—though there are plenty of other grounds for such criticism. Keyensian economic theory, which emerged in the 1930s, suggests that a major way of reducing the level of unemployment is for the government to run a deficit in its budget, perhaps by increasing the level of government expenditure. The deficit results in higher incomes for some sectors of the economy and the expenditure of these incomes generates additional economic activity leading to a higher demand for labour. The governments of the 1920s cannot be blamed for their ignorance of this theory, but if the theory is valid the relationship between government expenditure and unemployment would still hold, even though there was no general awareness of this relationship.

fronts, fronts moreover where the government, reacting to the pressure for economy, had already made significant reductions in its estimates. In the general atmosphere of retrenchment and economy the high aims of, for example, Fisher's Education Act of 1918 were largely abandoned. The Act—engineered by H. A. L. Fisher, the Oxford historian who served as President of the Board of Education in Lloyd George's governments—had promised wide-ranging and progressive changes which seemed likely to give Britain a coherent system of education. But it was little implemented. For example, few of the continuation schools—planned to provide part-time education for two years for those who left school at fourteen—were built and compulsory attendance at them rapidly disappeared. Similarly, house-building by local authorities under the Addison Act of 1919 was suspended in 1922.[6] In neither of these fields—nor in other areas such as the provision of public health facilties, which were also pruned—did the cuts and economies do more than temporarily halt the general trend of social progress. In education, after the Hadow Report of 1926, much effort was devoted to reorganising schools to implement the proposal that different types of secondary education should be provided after the age of eleven. In housing the patent shortages led to the passing of the Chamberlain Act of 1923 and the Wheatley Act of 1924 with their differing—and less extravagant—ways of providing the housing subsidies which had formed the basis of the Addison Act of 1919. The direction of the flow of social action towards the provision of more and better social services was largely irreversible:

6. Houses erected in Great Britain, 1920–1930 (Source: J. Ashworth, *Housing in Great Britain*, 1957, p. 34):

| Year | Local authorities | Private enterprise | | Total |
		Subsidy	Non-subsidy	
1919–20	576	139 ⎫		275,930
1920–21	16,786	13,328 ⎪	58,800	
1921–22	86,579	21,577 ⎬	approx.	approx.
1922–23	67,062	11,083 ⎭		
1923–24	19,582	4,534	69,396	93,516
1924–25	23,862	48,830	71,072	143,764
1925–26	49,508	66,569	68,254	184,331
1926–27	83,714	83,681	65,867	233,262
1927–28	120,494	77,725	62,479	260,698
1928–29	69,677	52,156	66,015	187,848
1929–30	73,268	53,825	93,099	220,192

none the less, the attitude of restrictive economy that dominated the 1920s tended to staunch this flow and impoverish the quality of British life at this time.

This squeeze on expenditure on social welfare emerges clearly from an examination of the categories of government expenditure during the 1920s. After 1922, by which time the total level of expenditure was flattening out at £750–800 million per annum—its apparent norm for the decade—the payment of debt charges usually absorbed at least 40 per cent, and a further 15 per cent was spent on defence.

An inappropriate industrial structure

The disturbances of war and the limited wisdom of policies which—in hindsight at least—seem misguided or even counter-productive, both contributed towards the economic difficulties of this period. They were overshadowed, however, by at least two basic, and closely related, long-run trends. These were the tendency for the nation's industrial structure to adapt itself too sluggishly to the changing needs of the twentieth century and for both the pattern and the performance of Britain's extenal trade to reflect this increasingly inappropriate balance.

Before 1913 the nation's industrial structure was still dominated by its nineteenth-century staples—coal, cotton, iron, and steel. In 1911 coal, textiles, and clothing on their own employed about one-fifth of the total occupied population, while the 1907 census of production indicated that about one-half of the net output in the manufacturing sector originated in coal, textiles, and iron and steel (including engineering and shipbuilding).[7] The same dominance by a relatively narrow range of industries is reflected even more strongly in Britain's foreign trade. Cotton yarn and manufactures alone accounted for one-quarter of the total value of Britain's commodity exports in 1910: the proportion rises to over one-half if exports of iron and steel, coal, and other textiles are added to those of cotton.[8]

The mere preponderance of these industries was, in itself, of no great significance or concern: after all, it was this pattern that had underlain Britain's towering industrial leadership in the nineteenth century. The problem arose because, even before 1914, it was becom-

7. Calculated from P. Deane and W. A. Cole, *British Economic Growth, 1688–1959*, 1964, Chapter IV, Tables 31 and 32; A. E. Kahn, *Britain in the World Economy*, 1946, pp. 65–9.

8. Deane and Cole, *op. cit.*, p. 31, Table 9.

ing increasingly clear that these industries formed a highly insecure base for future expansion. This is not to say that the pre-1914 pattern of industrial investment was therefore irrational. There was in these years a high level of demand overseas—especially in developing Empire countries—and this seemed to hold out good prospects for expansion in the staple industries most affected.

The demand was, it is true, partially fed by a strong upsurge of British capital export. But the high rate of British investment abroad —although perhaps over-stimulated because the London money market was better adapted for channelling investment abroad rather than at home[9]—was in general solidly based on the prospects of securing a good rate of return. The continued expansion of the staple industries before 1914, although unfortunate for the future, was based upon decisions which were reasonable at the time—if one accepts that business expectations are often based on quite short time-horizons, on overweighting current experience, and undervaluing real long-term prospects.

These prospects had been substantially dimmed by 1914. It was always inevitable that, as industrialisation spread, Britain's share of the world output of these staples would eventually decline: but the pace and extent of this decline between 1870 and 1914 were un-comfortably rapid. We have already seen (above, p. 12) that by the eve of the First World War both the United States and Germany had outstripped Britain in the production of pig-iron. It was still more disquieting that in the more expansionary sector of the industry—steel production—both the United States and Germany had sur-passed Britain by even greater margins. By 1913, moreover, Germany narrowly overtook Britain as an exporter of iron and steel products, and again it was clear that Britain fared least well in those sectors—structural steel and steel plates—for which world demand was most buoyant.[10]

In textiles British output was growing quite slowly between 1900 and 1914, while exports, in terms of volume though not of value, were almost stagnant during these years. None the less they continued to dominate total British exports. At first sight the situation in coal looked more promising. In terms of output, employment, and, especially, exports, coal was expanding very rapidly in the decade

9. As was indicated by the Macmillan Committee in 1931. Committee on Finance and Industry, *Minutes of Evidence*, Q 3511–16.

10. S. B. Saul, 'The Export Economy, 1870–1914', *Yorkshire Bulletin*, vol. 17, 1965, p. 15.

before 1914. Coal—exhibiting a trend quite the reverse of that of cotton—had, indeed, become steadily more important in Britain's commodity exports, providing in 1913 one-tenth of the total value of these. There were, however, strong signs (with hindsight they have become certainties) that the upsurge in the coal industry had by then largely run its course: productivity was declining and costs rising; foreign competition was growing more effective as the richest and most easily accessible British seams were worked out; the substitution of other fuels, especially oil, was slowly but unmistakably making headway. In 1913 no objective observer could have expected the most recent rates of growth to continue for long.

Importance of staple industries for exports

Thus in each of these major sectors there was much evidence—often stretching back several decades before 1914—that the expansionary tendencies of the past were slackening and might even be reversed. It was this aspect which aroused forebodings about the extent to which these sectors continued to dominate both Britain's industrial structure and her export trade.

These long-run tendencies contributed significantly to the economic ills of the 1920s. Their impact was most marked in the decline in export demand. Indeed, in the case of both coal and cotton, the decline in total output could be substantially attributed to the loss of export markets.[11] And because these industries loomed so large in the industrial structure the resultant unemployment formed a significant part of that more or less irreducible figure of one million unemployed that so blighted the 1920s. Indeed, for six of the major staple industries it was estimated that, in 1929, the unemployment

11. Output and exports of coal and cotton piece goods (Sources: Mitchell and Deane, *British Historical Statistics*, pp. 116, 119, 120; G. P. Jones and A. G. Pool, *A Hundred Years of Economic Development*, 1940, p. 287):

Cotton piece goods			Coal			
Year	Output m. sq. yds.	Exports m. sq. yds.	Year	Output m. tons	Exports (including bunkers) m. tons	Nos. employed (000s)
1912	8,050	6,913	1913	287	94	1,128
1924	6,026	4,444	1924	267	79	1,214
1930	3,320	2,407	1930	244	70	931

due to the decline in exports since 1913 was about ¾ million workers. This—or at least the presumed failure to re-absorb these workers in other sectors—would 'explain' much of the persistently high unemployment.[12]

Besides graphically illustrating the extent to which the economic difficulties of the decade were due to secular (i.e. long-term) trends, these industries also serve to show the importance of the disruptions of war. Wartime needs required the maintenance of a high level of activity in these industries while simultaneously cutting the links with major overseas markets. This made the eventual process of adjustment at once sharper and shorter. Both influences—the secular and the specific—stand out especially starkly in the case of the Indian market for British cotton goods. Before the First World War, Lancashire sent over 3,000 million square yards to India. The dominance of the Indian market (70 per cent of the total quantity of cotton goods in India came from Britain) was bound to decline as Indian home production increased: this was the long-run trend. The war, however, vastly stimulated Indian home production and—since India had been easily the largest single market for British cotton piece goods, taking over 40 per cent of British exports—this accelerated Lancashire's decline. In 1929 India was taking only two-fifths of the pre-war quantity from Britain and this slumped to less than one-quarter in 1930. In this market alone sales of over 2,000 million square yards a year had been lost in a very short period. It was partly because of influences such as these that—even in such comparatively good years for world trade as 1925–29—the value of British exports declined absolutely as well as relatively.

Difficulties of adjustment

In many respects then the basic problem of the British economy was to shift—on a massive scale—resources out of these basic industries and into sectors where there were favourable growth prospects. There were, however, also influences external to the British economy which made these adjustments more difficult at this time. There was a tendency for obstacles to international trade to increase. The Versailles settlement created a number of new countries, each of which was anxious to protect its industries by tariffs, while the industrial development which had been stimulated by war—in countries such as India and Brazil—also tended to be preserved by protection during

12. E. V. Francis, *Britain's Economic Strategy*, 1939, pp. 55–6.

the years of peace. In addition, there was, as we shall see later, (pp. 64–5), substantial agricultural over-production. This exercised a depressive effect upon many primary product prices—and hence upon the level of incomes in agricultural countries. As a result the demand of these countries for industrial products was less expansive than it had been before 1914—and this was especially serious for Britain because primary product countries had formed a large part of her pre-war market for exports.

Finally the vast network of inter-allied war debts and reparations payments also unsettled normal trading relations. As part of the war settlement the victors attempted to exact large sums as reparations from the defeated powers. The attempt finally collapsed in the early 1930s, but it was a source of continuous confusion, difficulty, and international bitterness throughout the preceding years. Germany was saddled initially with an obligation to pay the Allied powers some £6,500 million. Even apart from German resentment and unwillingness, it was an obligation which was extremely difficult—and perhaps impossible—to meet. Besides the size of the burden, payment ultimately involved large unrequited exports of German goods. These goods had first to be withheld from German consumers and then transferred overseas. But since Germany's creditors produced similar goods, they were reluctant either to accept these goods themselves or to have them displacing their own exports in other markets.

The whole problem was, in any case, vastly complicated because alongside it there was an intricate system of inter-allied war debts. Many of the continental allies owed substantial sums to the United States and to Britain. Britain, in her turn, was indebted to the United States. America, as the ultimate creditor, made strenuous efforts to collect these debts, but her attempts were more effective in arousing resentment than in producing money. The total effect was disruptive of normal trade, especially as the strains and uncertainties imposed by these various obligations unsettled the foreign exchange markets and bedevilled the attempts to restore a sound system of international finance.

Changes in the operation of the international trading system

Most of the substantial and repeated efforts at international economic co-operation that were made in the 1920s were aimed at reducing the obstacles to trade and minimising the impact of the legacy of the wartime financial settlements. They met with very limited success.

Even the World Economic Conference of 1927—meeting in the most favourable atmosphere of a generally buoyant level of world trade—could reduce tariff barriers only marginally, and then only for a very brief space of time. Also, Britain had centred her economic policy upon a return to the gold standard partly to stimulate a move towards more settled trading conditions. There were, however, powerful reasons—quite apart from the particular issue of the strain imposed by an over-valued pound—why the gold standard system of the 1920s was unable to operate as smoothly as it had before 1914. And these reasons form a strategic part of the explanation of the economic difficulties of these years.

In part the change came simply because Britain was less able to play its pre-war role. It is important to remember that before 1914 Britain had acted as the lynch-pin of the gold standard system. Sterling was the standard currency; and the London discount houses —dealing mainly in trade bills—were a major means of financing international trade, including trade in which Britain was not directly involved as either importer or exporter. This high degree of reliance on sterling required that there should be no doubt about the maintenance of its gold value, and also that sterling should not be a currency in short supply.

Before 1914 both these requirements were met. There was a universal acceptance of Britain's intention to maintain the gold value of sterling, and there was a solid basis—in terms of her strong creditor position—for Britain's ability to do so. Moreover, sterling was not a scarce currency. Britain's consistently unfavourable balance of visible trade ensured a steady flow of sterling to some major suppliers; and although the influence of invisible items—shipping, insurance, banking, and dividends—converted this into an overall favourable balance, the surplus was normally used to finance long-term investment overseas and hence made sterling available.

In the 1920s both Britain's intentions and her ability to operate this gold standard system were inevitably called in question. Her external credit position was decidedly weaker: some foreign assets—representing probably more than 10 per cent of the pre-war holdings —had been sold, while the uncertainties surrounding war debts were unsettling.[13] And although the balance of payments—apart from the

13. Britain was a net creditor in the tangled system of inter-allied war debts and hence this should perhaps have been a source of strength: but Britain always seemed more likely to pay than to be paid—and this was indeed the eventual outcome.

year of the general strike—continued to be favourable, the scale of the balance was small in relation to the position before 1914.

It seems likely that the value of long-term overseas investment in the latter half of the 1920s was greater than the surplus on current account.[14] Thus the financing of this overseas investment was partially dependent on the attraction of short-term funds to London. It was much more important, however, that London's normal pre-war situation of being a substantial creditor on short-term account disappeared during the war: it was this that really created the need to attract short-term funds to London. Before 1914 a mere slackening in the rate of lending overseas would bring in a flow of gold to London in payment of maturing bills: in the 1920s foreign short-term balances 'had to be wooed' in E. V. Morgan's words, 'with attractive interest rates', otherwise there was a strong danger that they would be withdrawn and thus depress the price of sterling.

Even apart from these weaknesses, Britain would have been less able to play her pre-war role because her pre-war dominance in international finance had disappeared. The United States had become increasingly important in world trade and a major source of international investment. Both tendencies inevitably increased the importance of New York as an international financial centre and as a rival to London. To a more limited extent Paris also gained ground over London in this respect, particularly towards the end of the decade when an under-valued franc had made the external financial position of France very strong indeed.

The mere multiplication of strategic financial centres reduced to some degree the efficiency of the gold standard system, but this was overshadowed by the extent to which New York was less suited than London had been for this purpose. No doubt, as some commentators emphasise, New York did not have the same expertise: but this on its own would not have been either important or long-lived. More fundamental was New York's relative insensitivity to trade movements. The New York money market continued to reflect the vast internal American economy much more than the external trading situation. The United States had become of major importance in world trade; but external trade formed only a small part of American economic activity. Against this background it naturally took some time for American attitudes and policies to become adjusted to the

14. A. E. Kahn, *Britain in the World Economy*, pp. 161–4; P. Deane and W. A. Cole, *British Economic Growth*, p. 37.

enhanced position of the United States in world trade and finance; certainly, this process was far from completed in the 1920s.

By the 1920s, moreover, the London money market had itself become much less responsive to trade movements. Before 1914 the London discount market was largely dominated by trade bills—Treasury bills were relatively insignificant. Thus the short-term market very quickly reflected trade trends. But by the 1920s the great growth of internal unfunded public debt—largely a legacy of war—had made Treasury bills more important in the market than trade bills. This in itself made the market less sensitive to movements in trade and the tendency was heightened because the Bank of England, in its manipulation of interest rates, was bound at least to consider that any decision to raise rates would increase the cost of servicing government debt.

Furthermore, to economise in gold which was expected to be scarce, the Genoa Conference of 1922 had recommended that countries should not reintroduce gold coins for the use of internal currency, and also that some countries could hold part of their currency reserve in the form of the currencies of those other countries which were tied to gold. Many countries thus held part of their reserves in the form of sterling balances. These represented a short-term liability for Britain, but Britain's liquid short-term funds were inadequate to meet all the claims which might arise. It was thus important that these balances—and other short-term foreign funds—should be retained in London.

This task was complicated because their owners were primarily interested, not in securing an income from their money, but in maintaining its gold value. Thus an increase in interest rates—if this was interpreted as a sign of the weakness of sterling—would be more likely to drive funds out than attract them in. The same was true of the so-called 'hot money'—the private capitalists' counterpart to the exchange funds of the various governments—since here, too, the prime concern of its owners was to maintain the capital value. Before 1914 short-term capital and its movement were closely related to trading needs. The sterling balances and 'hot money' of the 1920s (and later) exhibited no such relation.

All these tendencies and changes made the operation of the gold standard, after its restoration from 1925 onwards, much less smooth and apparently automatic than it had been before 1914. The position was, moreover, further exacerbated because the shocks of war, and the post-war inflations and social disturbances, had eroded another less tangible but no less fundamental base of the earlier situation: the long absence of major wars and an expectation of continuing stability.

Were the 1920s years of economic depression?

There seems, then, to be no shortage of possible explanations for the disappointing performance of the British economy: the effects of war and the distorting influence of the powerful post-war boom; inadequate or misconceived policies; unfavourable long-run trends; and significant changes in the operation of the international trading system. Many explanations, then; but it has been suggested recently that there is nothing to explain.

It has been argued that the tendency to concentrate attention upon the plight of a small range of staple industries, upon external trade—the volume of exports even in the best years of 1925–29 was only four-fifths of that of 1913—and upon the level of unemployment, gives a distorted view of the 1920s. If instead attention is concentrated upon the overall growth of output, and trends in industrial productivity, a much more promising picture emerges.[15] Put in its most extreme form this view claims that the economic progress made by Britain in the 1920s was at least as favourable as that of the rest of Europe and was markedly better than Britain's pre-1913 performance. The decade of the 1920s, therefore, marked 'a watershed' and 'ranks as one of the most buoyant periods in our recent history'.[16]

This reappraisal appears rather over-enthusiastic. Contemporaries certainly seem to have had little feeling that they were managing their economic affairs so much better than in Edwardian times. Indeed, most articulate opinion, reflecting the views of the wealthy and relatively wealthy, continued to look back nostalgically to the glittering mirage of an Edwardian golden age. The inarticulate majority were more apt to measure the present not against the past but against the hopes which had been raised during and after the war. They were less aware of any marked economic progress and more conscious of the inadequate housing and of the pervading sense of insecurity that arose when one in ten was always out of work. None

15. D. H. Aldcroft, 'Economic Progress in Britain in the 1920s', *Scot. Jnl. of Pol. Econ.*, 13, 1966, p. 297 and comment by N. K. Buxton and rejoinder by Aldcroft in *ibid.*, 14, 1967, pp. 175 and 187; D. H. Aldcroft, 'Economic Growth in Britain in the Inter-war Years: A Re-assessment', *Econ. Hist. Rev.* 20, 1967, p. 311; J. A. Dowie, 'Growth in the inter-war period: some more arithmetic', *Econ. Hist. Rev.*, 21, 1968, p. 93.

16. Aldcroft, *loc. cit.*, 13, 1966.

the less it is fairly clear that industrial output rose in the 1920s at an annual rate greater than that of the immediate pre-war years, and that this trend was still more marked for industrial productivity.[17] Perhaps too much significance should not be attached to this since it should be noted that the growth rate between 1899 and 1913 was exceptionally low by nineteenth century standards.

Economic gains of the 1920s

Perhaps even more important than these statistical abstractions, is the fact that controversy over the rate of economic progress in the 1920s serves as a lively and necessary reminder of the important economic advances of the time. These were usually less obtrusive than the signs of decline: a new factory opening—especially as starts were often on a modest scale—tended to attract less attention than an old one closing and perhaps throwing many people out of a job. Such expansions were often associated with the so-called new industries.

These will be dealt with rather more fully later. Here it only needs to be noticed that, besides the decline of coal and cotton, the 1920s saw significant growth in such industries as aircraft and motor vehicles, rayon and electrical products. There was also quite substantial technical change: new inventions, new methods, changes in organisation. Some of these sprang more or less directly from the stimulus given by the war—aircraft, motor vehicles (especially trucks), automatic welding, and the establishment, in 1916, of the Department of Scientific and Industrial Research. But there were others. During the decade, for example, Britain—Courtauld's—was in the van of world developments in rayon;[18] in shipbuilding the changes in engine and

17. Annual percentage rates of growth of U.K. gross domestic product, 1856–1962 (Source: R. C. O. Matthews, 'Aspects of post-war growth', p. 3. Figures for 1924–29 from Dowie, 'Growth in inter-war period', *Econ. Hist. Review*, p. 108):

	Real G.D.P.	G.D.P. per man year
1856–99	2·0	1·1
1899–1913	1·1	0·1
1924–37	2·3	1·1
1924–29	2·3	0·9
1948–62	2·5	1·9

18. J. Harrop, 'The Growth of the Rayon Industry in the Inter-war Years', *Yorks. Bull.*, 20, 1968, p. 71; D. C. Coleman, *Courtaulds: an Economic and Social History*, Vol. II: *Rayon*, 1969.

hull design were sufficiently revolutionary to generate some demand despite the vast world surplus of ships; and similar examples could be cited in the fields of radio, new alloy metallurgy, and electrical engineering.

At the same time, the decade witnessed the spread of several significant, but more general, methods—the use of conveyor belts, of more exact measurement, of faster machine tools. In addition, there were many changes in industrial organisation. One of the key words of the decade was rationalisation, although this process was more muted in Britain than in such countries as Germany and the United States. Often what was implied was nothing more than old-fashioned monopolisation and restriction of competition, but in many sectors this was a necessary preliminary to the closing down of redundant capacity, and the concentration of production in fewer units where economies of scale could be exploited.

Difficulties of interpretation

However, the problem with trends such as these—important but nebulous—is to know just how significant they were. The multiplication of examples and illustrations may be deceptive or misleading. It is, for example, quite definite that there was more research directly and indirectly related to industry in Britain in the 1920s than there had been before the war; but it is still possible—it was the view of the Balfour Committee on Industry and Trade in 1927—that Britain had none the less fallen still further behind the United States in this respect. The statistics of industrial production and productivity are intended to indicate whether these favourable trends outweighed the less happy trends of the decade. The figures seem less nebulous, more definite, more objective.

But perhaps no less deceptive. Inevitably the figures themselves do give rise to some difficulties because of the limitations of the data on which they are based, the choice of base years, and the weighting adopted. Thus, for example, the picture swings fairly sharply from one indicating impressive economic progress if the calculations are made using 1913 as a base, to being generally unfavourable if 1920 is used. There are clear objections to both. The period between 1913 and 1929 can hardly be said to be the 1920s. The year 1920 is unsatisfactory for international comparisons because Britain had by then much more completely recovered from the war than had most other European countries, and for domestic comparisons because

1920 had a much lower unemployment level than 1929. Both these difficulties can be avoided by taking 1924 as a base, but there are major drawbacks in defining the 1920s as the period between 1924 and 1929.

These statistical reservations, while a source of much academic sport, should not be exaggerated. It may be cautiously accepted that the figures suggest that industrial production—and especially productivity—grew more rapidly in the 1920s than in the immediate pre-war years. There is, however, more basis for unease about some of the conclusions that seem to be drawn from this fact. The implication is that the performance of the economy was satisfactory and the growth rate commendable. This verdict must be strongly tempered by at least two observations.

First, contemporary awareness of this economic progress was very muted. As Youngson puts it: 'Scarcely anyone thought, in the later 1920s, that they were living through the closing years of the upswing of a trade cycle.'[19] In 1925 there had seemed to be some basis for optimism: the Dawes Plan of 1924 had provided a feasible settlement of the problem of reparations payments; the Locarno Pact had lowered international tensions; Britain, Germany, and others had returned to the gold standard. Everything suggested that the difficult period of post-war reconstruction was over and 'normal' progress would be resumed. But in 1929—statistically the best year for the economy—the pervading attitude was one of anxiety and doubt. Even the outgoing Conservative Government did not base their election campaign on a confident pride in their economic achievement. Perhaps contemporary opinion was more than usually shortsighted; but it is still *their* economic welfare that was supposed to be thriving.

Secondly, the achievement of growth has also to be viewed in the light of its distribution. In this respect the persistence of a 10 per cent unemployment rate—Pigou's 'intractable million'—hung heavily over the decade. It was this issue that dominated the election of 1929. It was this which for many families constituted the economic reality of the 1920s.

Unemployment and productivity

Perhaps one of the most interesting economic problems of the 1920s, —indeed of the inter-war years as a whole—concerns the nature of the

19. A. J. Youngson, *The British Economy, 1920–57*, 1960, p. 75.

relationship between the level of unemployment and the clear indications of rising industrial productivity and output. There were, of course, other factors at work—technical developments, for example, and the rise of new industries. The relatively small increase in net industrial investment during the 1920s suggests, however, that it is unlikely that the pace of technical innovation was fast enough to account for much of the increases in output and productivity. Nor is it realistic to attribute the favourable trend wholly to the emergence of the so-called new industries: in the 1920s any reasonable definition of new industries makes them too small to carry the weight of a general explanation.

There are, however, several reasons for thinking that the existence of heavy unemployment may have contributed towards the favourable trends in output and productivity, although it is difficult to say how large this contribution was. Part of this difficulty arises because unemployment seems to have been both a cause and an effect of the rising productivity. An effect because higher productivity and the process of rationalisation—other things being equal—tended to reduce the demand for labour. A cause because unemployment reduced the industrial strength of organised labour[20] particularly after 1926—and eased the way for the introduction of new methods and greater flexibility. Labour productivity seems to have risen more rapidly than average in the old declining industry of coal-mining, perhaps partly for this reason. The high level of unemployment also meant that resources—particularly labour—were being released for transfer from old to new industries—and perhaps this meant transfer from sectors of low productivity towards those of higher productivity.

This transfer of resources was the essential prerequisite for the major alteration of the balance of the industrial structure that had clearly become necessary by the 1920s. The maintenance of a large pool of unemployed labour may not be the most efficient way of effecting such a transfer, but its existence is likely to have some

20. Trade union membership (Source: Mitchell and Deane, *British Historical Statistics*, p. 68):

	Number (in millions)
1920	8·3
1925	5·5
1930	4·8

beneficial effects on the general level of productivity. Some part of the statistical progress of the decade would therefore be derived more or less directly from what many regard as its major economic failure.

Chapter 3

Goodbye to All That: the Economic Collapse, 1929–32

World depression

If there is some doubt about the direction in which the economic signposts were pointing up to 1929, there is no ambiguity over their meaning for the next few years. Nearly all the indices moved downwards—and this was not merely a slackening in the rate of growth but a decline in absolute levels. Between 1929 and 1932 national income fell by about 13 per cent, fixed capital formation by 20 per cent, manufacturing production by 10 per cent, retail prices by 13 per cent, while the proportion of insured workers who were unemployed more than doubled to over 20 per cent.[1] There were unequivocally years of economic depression and decline.

Nor is there much doubt that the source of these disasters lay largely outside the British economy, which mainly reflected—usually in a more moderate way—general world trends. The international depression which set in from around 1929 was unprecedented in its magnitude and intensity. Sober observers wondered if the entire system would collapse. A distinguished economic historian, writing in 1932, closed his survey of two centuries of British development

1. Some major economic indicators, 1929–32. (Source: *The British Economy: Key Statistics, 1900–1966*, 1967, London and Cambridge Economic Service):

	Net national income current prices £m.	Gross domestic product 1958 prices £m.	Gross domestic capital formation current prices £m.	Total domestic expenditure £m.	Imports value c.i.f. £m.	Exports value f.o.b. £m.	Manufacturing production 1958 = 100	Unemployment per cent*
1929	4,147	12,233	442	4,999	1,221	729	46·4	10·4
1932	3,614	11,276	347	4,559	702	365	41·6	22·1

* The unemployment figures refer not to the proportion of the total labour force which was out of work, but to the proportion of insured workers who were unemployed. The number covered by the Insurance Acts varied from time to time but basically during the inter-war years they covered nearly all manual workers and most low-paid white-collar workers.

with the words: 'If western capitalism founders in our time, posterity will surely give as its verdict, "Suicide, whilst of unsound mind".'[2]

It is of the utmost importance that the imaginative effort be made to realise how widespread the breakdown was and how overwhelming it appeared to contemporaries. An estimate for twenty-four of the most important countries in the international economy showed that nearly all of them suffered—within the space of three or four years—a decline in national income in money terms ranging from one-quarter to over one-half. World manufacturing production fell by 30 per cent while the number of unemployed in the main industrial countries in 1932 approached 30 million, half of whom were in the United States. World agricultural prices fell by 60 per cent.[3]

The depression was thus both calamitous and—almost—universal. The Soviet Union, which had largely insulated itself from the international economy, was little affected although, since these were the years of the major and bloody clash between the régime and the peasantry, it had sufficient internal troubles of its own. The United States was the major centre of distress. Wholesale prices there fell by a third and production was more than halved between 1929 and 1932. A slump of this magnitude was bound to have severe repercussions on the world economy, especially as American imports fell in much the same proportion as American income, while the United States had also been the main source of international lending before 1929.

Nearly one-half of the total imports into the United States between 1926 and 1930 consisted of primary products—foodstuffs and raw materials. The American collapse thus fell with devastating force on the major primary producing countries. These countries found themselves faced with acute balance of payments difficulties, and already by 1930 eight of these—Argentina, Australia, Bolivia, Brazil, Hungary, New Zealand, Paraguay, and Venezuela—had been forced to devalue their currencies as primary product prices plummeted. In the absence of any effective international action, such countries were forced to try to defend themselves from the effects of the depression by placing restrictions on the level of their imports. Indeed, the barriers to trade rose generally—especially after the dislocations of the international financial crisis (see below, pp. 67–9)

2. C. R. Fay, *Great Britain from Adam Smith to the Present Day*, 1932 (3rd edition), p. 451.

3. League of Nations, *The Transition from War to Peace*, Part I, 1943, p. 21; and *Industrialisation and World Trade*, 1945, pp. 134–5.

were added to the general malaise. The value of world trade fell by nearly two-thirds—even more than world production—between 1929 and 1933.[4]

The decline of American lending was particularly crucial for Germany. As part of the post-war settlement, Germany had been saddled with the commitment to pay substantial reparations for the damage caused to other countries by the war. Although the scale of these had been progressively reduced in the 1920s, in the face of Germany's inability and unwillingness to meet these obligations, they remained a formidable burden. A significant proportion of the payments which Germany did make before 1929 was financed by loans from the United States, which were also an important source for the capital required for German industrial investment. The economic resurgence of Germany after 1925 was thus heavily dependant upon the flow of American capital—activity in the German economy fell drastically as this flow dwindled from 1928 onwards. The reparations problem was eventually solved by the virtual abandonment of reparation payments after the Lausanne Agreement of 1932, which followed the moratorium on war debts and reparations which President Hoover had called for in 1929. But this was too late. Production in Germany in mid-1932 was only half its 1929 level: this industrial dislocation with its accompanying social upheaval—symbolised by the 6 million unemployed—was leading towards the establishment of the Nazi régime.

The depression of the early thirties was, indeed, nearly everywhere more marked than in Britain. Perhaps it is not surprising, therefore, that the major causes of the world economic crisis were also to be found outside Britain: in the general trends in the international economy and in the impact of events in the United States.

The unfavourable trends in the world economy

The virtual breakdown in the international economy in the early 1930s clearly derived in part from the serious shortcomings—already outlined (pp. 51–5)—of the post-1925 gold standard mechanism. Even more fundamental perhaps was the general atmosphere of political and economic instability and insecurity: the pre-1914 system had depended very largely on confidence in the continuance of peace, or at least on the avoidance of major conflicts.

4. From $68 billion to $24 billion. League of Nations, *World Economic Survey, 1933–34*, 1934, p. 187.

The years between 1925 and 1929 were the nearest the inter-war years came to recapturing these conditions. Even so, the pleas of the World Economic Conference of 1927—the heyday of international economic and political co-operation in the inter-war period—fell almost entirely on stony ground. Nearly all nations welcomed, in the abstract, the call for a reduction in tariffs, but 'as with national armaments some years later, so with national tariffs, it proved impossible to find an acceptable general principle on which reductions by different States . . . might be based'.[5]

More specifically, the 1920s was a period of mounting crisis in world agriculture. Some commodities fared reasonably well—raw materials and some animal products—but for the producers of many basic crops, especially wheat and sugar, the decade was one of almost continuous difficulty. There was marked over-production in the sense that, despite increases in stocks, prices tended to fall—gently for a few years after 1925, but precipitately in 1929.[6] On the supply side this had two main sources. Firstly, the disruptions of war increased the demands for many raw materials and some foodstuffs, and at the same time partially cut off supplies from the normal producing countries. The encouragement thus given to new producing areas often survived—usually with government help—the post-war return to normal trading channels. Secondly, there were important forces—especially the spreading use of such mechanical methods as the tractor, and the biological advances producing new seed strains—making for increased agricultural productivity. Both these influences tended to increase world agricultural output.

But while supply was thus expanding there were strong forces holding down the growth of demand. Thus, for example, there was a tendency for substitutes for some primary products to be developed (such as man-made fibres and artificial rubber). Much more important, the slowing down of population growth in industrial countries—the main source of the world market for agriculture—acted as a check on the rate of growth of demand for foodstuffs, as did the tendency for people—as incomes rose—to spend a smaller proportion of their income on food (the so-called Engel's law).

The resultant dwindling prices and rising stocks inevitably created difficult balance of payments problems for many countries—Australia, Brazil, Cuba, New Zealand, Argentina, Egypt, Greece—

5. League of Nations, *Commercial Policy in the Inter-War Period*, 1942, p. 128.
6. By the end of 1929 agricultural prices were only two-thirds of the average level of 1923–25. J. B. Condliffe, *The Commerce of Nations*, 1951, p. 488.

which were dependent on exports of primary products. These strains were tolerable—or at least were contained—as long as industrial activity continued at a high level, and as long as American foreign investment continued to tide the agricultural countries over their balance of payments difficulties. The economic collapse of the United States after 1929 was thus crucial: it removed both of these conditions, and set off a catastrophic decline in agricultural prices in 1930, a decline that did much to extend and deepen the general world depression.

Unfavourable trends in the economy of the United States

Thus it was the abrupt ending of the boom in the United States which was the decisive influence. For most of the 1920s America had been riding a wave of high prosperity. The prolonged nature of this expansion, in relation to previous experience, and the extraordinary stability of prices, encouraged the belief that the disruptions of the trade cycle had been overcome. In 1929 all this was ended. The dramatic intensity of the stock market collapse of 24 October—followed by an even worse day on 29 October—in itself had a profoundly depressive psychological impact.

Some part of the responsibility for the intensity of the speculative fever—and hence for the enormity of the ultimate disappointment—rests with the American banking authorities. The Federal Reserve System managers did not act soon enough or strongly enough to cut back the credit which was feeding the stock market boom. In part this was because they were more concerned to pursue a policy of keeping the general price level stable, and in part it was to assist the Bank of England to attract short-term funds by keeping the New York interest rate below that of London. It may be doubted anyway whether small changes in interest rates would have been effective in face of the bloated expectations of the stock market speculators.

Much more important was the fact that the major attractions which had made for a high and sustained level of investment in the United States during the 1920s were running out of steam. The development of new industries and new techniques—both of which were symbolised in the rapid growth of the automobile industry under the application of mass production methods—had provided much of the incentive for industrial investment after 1921. By 1929 the most obvious and most favourable investment opportunities were—temporarily—exhausted, and most of the indicators of industrial activity had already fallen off before the stock market crash. Of particular importance was the decline in building activity. This had been very high for much of the decade, helping to sustain a buoyant level of aggregate demand: its decline in 1929 thus undermined one of the pillars of the previous expansion.

These factors—the repercussions of the stock market crash, the temporary exhaustion of investment opportunities, and the end of the building boom—not only explain the American economic downturn in 1929: they also play a crucial part in accounting for the severity and length of the depression which followed in the United States. In addition, the economy was burdened with a high degree of indebtedness, the real weight of which increased as prices fell, and which acted as a deterrent both to more consumption spending and more investment.

Indebtedness within the economy took several main forms. Among consumers generally, for example, there was a heavy weight of hire-purchase debt.[7] The building boom of the 1920s meant, moreover, that there was a generally high level of mortgage indebtedness, while in agriculture much debt had been incurred to finance the war and immediate post-war expansion and this became largely insupportable as agricultural prices fell and industrial activity declined. All this contributed to the extensive bank failures of the early 1930s— over 5,000 banks failed in the years 1930–32 and over 4,000 in the single year of 1933—and the shock greatly sapped confidence and raised for a time real fears that the entire structure of economic activity in the United States was crumbling.[8]

7. Instalment buying had first emerged as a major phenomenon in the United States in the 1920s with the great growth in the importance of expensive consumer durable goods (cars, refrigerators, washing machines, etc.). By 1929, 13 per cent of all retail sales in the United States were made on this basis; but the ability of consumers to meet their accumulated commitments faltered as incomes fell and unemployment rose. These difficulties then led to sharp falls in consumer demand.

8. *Historical Statistics of the United States*, Washington, 1960, p. 636. Bank failures—even in normal times—were fairly commonplace in the United States, partly because of the existence of large numbers of small, independent banks. Even so the banking crisis of the early thirties was on an altogether different scale, not only because of the number of failures but also because many very large and apparently sound institutions were only saved by the imposition—by State and Federal governments—of extensive bank holidays. The general weakness of the structure of the American banking system thus contributed towards the depression in the economy.

Effects on other countries

The effect of all this on the outside world was catastrophic for two main reasons. Firstly, because American trade was so important in total world trade: in 1929 the United States was the world's largest exporter (15·8 per cent of total world exports) and second only to Britain as an importer. Thus any decline in the level of activity in America was bound to have widespread effects. Secondly, the United States had become the largest creditor nation and a substantial network of international credit depended on the continuance of American loans. Indeed, even before the crash, the internal movements of the American economy had already created problems for the outside world as American funds were diverted from foreign investment to feed the domestic stock market speculation.

After 1929 the dollar receipts of the outside world fell with alarming rapidity. By 1932 the dollars available to other countries had fallen by $5,000 million to only one-third of their 1929 level, and debtors everywhere were faced with acute balance of payments difficulties. These countries had to reduce their imports and this implied reductions in exports from other countries, which thus had *their* national incomes depressed leading to cuts in *their* imports . . . and so on in a declining spiral. The volume of world trade fell by some 60 per cent between 1929 and 1932.

The international financial crisis

These conditions led inexorably to an overwhelming international financial crisis. The vast maladjustments arising from war debts, reparations, and mounting deficits by primary producing nations had been held at bay by widespread international lending. In particular—since German reparations payments were the largest single problem—American loans to Germany had enabled Germany to meet her commitments. As these loans dwindled and virtually disappeared, major difficulties of international liquidity developed. Everywhere creditors were attempting to convert their assets into cash (gold or some apparently safe currency): many countries and institutions, as well as individuals, were unable to meet these demands. A substantial number of agricultural producing countries—mainly in Latin America and Australasia—had already been forced to depreciate their currencies in 1929 and 1930. In May 1931 the Austrian

Credit Anstalt Bank closed its doors; in July the German Danat Bank followed suit.

The closure of these banks precipitated a major international financial crisis. The pressure of this crisis tended, moreover, to concentrate upon London. There were several reasons for this. It was known that throughout the spring of 1931 the City and the Bank of England, attempting to avert the collapse in central Europe, had continued lending in Germany and Austria while Paris and New York were withdrawing their support. It was thought, therefore, that London must have lost substantial financial assets when the German collapse occurred. London had, in any event, become a precarious financial centre and, particularly in times of crisis, creditors are always anxious to withdraw their funds from any centre where there is any question as to their safety.

In 1931, the substantial gold reserves held in Paris and New York made these centres seem sound. But, as we have already seen,[9] London's position was much more problematical. The continuance of Britain's long-term investment overseas in the 1920s had depended upon the attraction of short-term foreign funds to London. When, as in 1931, these funds were being withdrawn from London, the long-term nature of British lending made it difficult to meet this drain by liquidating British assets overseas. Similarly the gold exchange standard meant that many countries held part of their international reserves in the form of short-term claims on London or New York. In a time of crisis they tended to convert these claims into gold.

Britain's total overseas assets were much in excess of the claims upon her; but her reserves of gold and other easily liquidated assets were constrained. A basic principle of banking is to hold sufficient reserves to meet any likely calls for cash. It is doubtful if London— as an international banking centre—was ever in this position during the period of the restored gold standard after 1925: it is certain that it was not when the international rush for liquidity concentrated on sterling in the summer of 1931.

It is true, as indicated above (pp. 61 ff.), that the main pressures acting on the British economy during these years came from outside. Equally clearly, however, these external pressures were acting upon a system which was highly vulnerable. The vulnerability of London—arising from Britain's weakened international trading and financial position—was still further increased because the other

9. See above, pp. 52–5.

major financial centres, New York and Paris, made very little contribution to international financial liquidity. Indeed, both France and the United States were net importers of capital in 1931. This meant that they were withdrawing their funds from overseas, driving people in the countries affected to look for alternative funds and to liquidate any foreign assets that they might hold. The pressure on London was thus increased.

London eventually received—in two bites—some financial assistance from Paris and New York. The favourable effects of these additions to Britain's liquid reserves on overseas confidence in London was, however, reduced by the obvious hesitation and reluctance with which these loans were provided. They were, in any case, insufficient. At the beginning of August the Bank of England received a credit of foreign exchange to the equivalent of £50 million from Paris and New York; by the end of the month this had been swept away—and with it went the minority Labour Government. A second credit equivalent to £80 million was equally ineffective, and rapidly evaporated. On 21 September Britain formally left the gold standard.

The responsibility of the Labour Government

The causes of the crisis were not all external, of course. The basic structural weakness of the British economy was an important factor—but it was a factor which had operated throughout the post-war period. More immediate is the possibility that it was the socialistic policies of a Labour government which fatally undermined confidence abroad. It is difficult to see much evidence for this. The government could certainly be reasonably accused of a strong tendency to let matters drift, and of an ineptitude greater than could be justified by its lack of a parliamentary majority. But it was persistent in its attempts to continue the operation of the gold standard system and to maintain the Churchillian sterling parity; and it eschewed—in sharp contrast to almost all other countries, and particularly the United States—any imposition of trade restrictions. Indeed, with Philip Snowden at the Treasury interpreting his watchdog duties with a greater and more puritanical zeal than his Conservative predecessors, very little reform was possible.

The charge of government extravagance was most influentially summarised in the report of the Committee on National Expenditure (the May Committee) in August 1931. The effect of the report of this committee is discussed below (p. 70). For the moment the point to notice is that the assertion of government extravagance really centred almost exclusively in the rising cost of unemployment benefit. The government's contribution to this was that, in the Unemployment Insurance Act of 1930, it slightly improved the benefits and made it rather easier to prove entitlement. This certainly contributed to the extra cost, although the major cause was, of course, the mounting level of unemployment that had its source in the general world depression.

It still seems unlikely that the deficit in the unemployment fund was the prime cause of the outflow of reserves. Even if we were to assume that the unemployment deficit had been much smaller, would this have stemmed the run on London? It is difficult to believe so. Certainly after the collapse of the Labour Government and the imposition of budgetary economies—mainly cuts in unemployment benefits and in the pay of government employees—the pressure on sterling, after only a very short pause, became even more marked. No doubt the *belief* that a Labour government was less sound contributed to the difficulties. Basically, however, confidence disappeared because of the underlying vulnerability of London in face of the unprecedented pressure caused by the collapse of agricultural prices, and the withdrawal of French and American credits.

None the less, in a crisis matters of timing are vital and the reluctance of the Labour Government to impose cuts in government expenditure in the weeks before its members resigned on 24 August certainly intensified the difficulties. But even here a much sharper shock to confidence came from the publication of the Macmillan and May Reports. The Macmillan Committee on Finance and Industry had been appointed as far back as November 1929. It was mainly concerned, and its report mainly dealt with, essentially long-run issues on which it was moderately reassuring, and was mildly revolutionary in its encouragement to greater state intervention. But it was incidentally unfortunate in two respects: it documented, and even exaggerated, the extent to which London's short-term liabilities exceeded its assets; and it did so on 13 July, just after the collapse of the German banks had, as we have seen, concentrated pressure on London.

The May Committee on National Expenditure had been appointed in February 1931 specifically to examine the short-run difficulty—and as a means of allowing the government to postpone the need to take unpleasant decisions. The publication of its report on 1 August —drawing attention to and, indeed, overstating the likely emergence of a budget deficit—was even more damaging. The Committee forecast a budget deficit of some £120 million unless there was an increase in taxation and a substantial reduction in government expenditure, especially in government payments to the unemployed. It was disagreement in the Cabinet as to how far the May Committee's proposals should be implemented that was the immediate cause of the fall of the Labour Government. Perhaps Snowden had hoped to use its alarmist diagnosis to secure his party's agreement to its disagreeable prescriptions of rigid economy; but in the atmosphere of August 1931 it should have been obvious that its major impact would be to produce the decline in confidence which its prescriptions were supposed to cure.

The Labour Government was replaced by the so-called National Government—which was still, for a time, led by Ramsay MacDonald and in which Philip Snowden continued to serve as Chancellor, but which was dominated by Conservatives. The change brought only a temporary respite. A fresh loan was obtained from France and the United States, and many of the recommendations of the May Committee were embodied in Snowden's autumn budget of 10 September. The alteration in the complexion and, to some degree, the intentions of the British government could, however, do little to halt the general crisis in the international economy, a crisis which—as we have seen—had its major origins outside Britain. Hence the outflow of gold from Britain continued and was accelerated when the proposed cuts in pay for the Navy provoked some protest among naval units at Invergordon, protests which were reported as a mutiny and further undermined foreign confidence in sterling. This episode undoubtedly affected the precise timing of Britain's abandonment of the gold standard—which took place on 21 September 1931—but there is no convincing reason for thinking that, without it, Britain's currency would have remained much longer tied to gold at the 1925 parity.

Once an event has happened it tends to take on an, often spurious, air of inevitability. Britain's eventual abandonment of the gold standard does really seem to have been unavoidable;[10] but, once

10. Even here, however, it must be remembered that Montagu Norman, the courteous dictator of the Bank of England, was crossing the Atlantic when the decision was taken by his deputies. He did not realise that this step had been taken until he arrived at Liverpool and was then furious with his subordinates. Perhaps if he had been in London earlier the decision might have been different. Andrew Boyle, *Montagu Norman*, 1967, p. 268; Thomas Jones, *A Diary with Letters*, 1954, p. 32.

done, its effects were much less catastrophic than the predictions and the desperate attempts to avoid it had led people to expect. These effects can be looked at under three broad headings: the effects on Britain's external trade; the effects on the international economy; and the effects on Britain's internal economy.

The gold standard abandoned: effects on Britain's external trade

The evidence suggests that leaving the gold standard had, at least in the short run, a favourable influence on Britain's external trading position. The external value of the pound fell fairly sharply to the end of 1931,[11] increasing the relative costs of imports and decreasing the relative costs of exports. This was partially offset as a number of other countries, particularly in Scandinavia, the Dominions, and the Empire, followed Britain's lead. Still, British exports secured a sudden and significant price advantage over a number of competitors, and this was especially important because the pound had been previously over-valued. There was a release of pressure, and this advantage was not diminished by any strong tendency for British prices to rise.

Despite the inflationary effects of higher import costs, British wholesale prices showed only a very modest increase, and retail prices remained steady. British exports continued to decline—the sharp falls in world trade made this largely unavoidable—but the stimulus given by devaluation considerably reduced the rate of decline. On the other hand, the relative increase in the price of imports reduced to some extent British demand for them, especially for manufactures, the imports of which fell substantially.[12] The British demand for some imports, particularly food, was relatively inelastic and hence the impact of devaluation on its own would have been to push up the total cost of these imports.

This tendency was, however, offset by two major considerations: a number of Britain's food suppliers had in fact depreciated their currencies along with sterling, while, more generally, the world prices of primary products continued to fall. These various trends are not easy to quantify, but a favourable overall effect emerges fairly

11. The gold standard parity of $4·86 to the £ fell to around $3·30 at the end of 1931, but rose thereafter.
12. The value of manufactured imports in 1932 was 45 per cent less than in 1931. Calculated from *The British Economy: Key Statistics, 1900–66*, 1967, p. 14.

clearly.[13] Between 1931 and 1933 the value of British visible exports had fallen less than 10 per cent: the value of visible imports had fallen by more than 20 per cent. At the same time the sharply unfavourable balance of payments on current account of 1931 (−£104 million) was halved in 1932 and eliminated the following year. No doubt this result was partly due to the greatly increased degree of protection which was introduced by the National Government as an emergency measure in 1931 and given a more permanent form in March 1932 by the Import Duties Act;[14] but this large-scale extension of protection was greatly facilitated because Britain had already left the gold standard.

The gold standard abandoned: effects on the international economy

In most countries the revival of internal economic activity was perceptible after 1932 and continued upwards to a peak in 1937. There was then a brief recession which was reversed in 1938 as many countries began to be affected by the rising demand for armaments. In some countries—like Germany and Japan—production for war purposes meant that the level of activity continued to rise even during the general recession of 1937.

The strength of the revival varied in different countries. It was, for example, relatively strong in Britain and Germany and relatively weak in the United States and France.[15] But the trends in world

13. Britain's terms of trade (defined as export prices expressed as a percentage of import prices) rose very sharply from 115 in 1929 to 140 in 1933 (1913 = 100). Although they fell away a little after this, Britain's terms of trade were persistently more favourable in the 1930s than they had been in the 1920s. The figures (see A. E. Kahn, *Great Britain in the World Economy*, 1946, p. 153) were:

1929	1930	1931	1932	1933	1934	1935	1936	1937	1938
115	122	134	135	140	136	134	130	124	133

14. This, with a number of specified exemptions, imposed a general customs duty of 10 per cent, and after the first report of the Import Duties Advisory Committee in April there was a general tariff of 20 per cent on manufactured goods. Soon about half of Britain's imports were liable to duty of between 10 and 20 per cent.

15. Indices of industrial production in various countries, 1929, 1932, and 1937:

	1929	1932	1937
Britain	100	84	124
Germany	100	53	117
United States	100	53	103
France	100	72	82

trade, although they were also upward, were less vigorous. The operation of the international economy was, indeed, severely constrained throughout the thirties. The tariff barriers which had been raised in response to the world crisis remained high for the rest of the decade. In addition, various other forms of trade restriction—particularly the use of import quotas and exchange control—tended to be employed. These factors partly explain why the recovery in world production was imperfectly reflected in world trade.[16]

The disruption of the international financial mechanism also inhibited the growth of trade. In this respect the abandonment of the gold standard by Britain was a major and fundamental event: it meant that the chances of an early restoration of a genuinely international economy were greatly dimmed; and it dramatically symbolised—since Britain alone had seemed fully committed to this ideal—the abandonment of a belief in the overriding benefit of a system of free multi-lateral trade.

It is sometimes suggested[17] that from about 1934 or 1935, once the worst of the crisis had passed, the various measures taken by individual countries—tariffs, exchange control, import quotas, and so on—to protect themselves against the general chaos should have been dismantled. This would, it is implied, have permitted a more general revival in trade to the benefit of all. There is no doubt, as we have seen, that the level of world trade lagged substantially behind world production during the 1930s.

There is much less certainty, however, that this lag arose only because of the restrictions on trade. The crushing nature of the world depression and of the financial collapse had undermined confidence in the benefits of a generally free and multilateral trading system. Particularly after the devaluation of the dollar in 1933, and the resounding failure of the World Economic Conference held in London in the same year, there was no reality in the hope that the removal of trade barriers would lead to a restoration of the inter-

16. Indices of world trade and world production, 1929, 1932, and 1937:

	1929	1932	1937
World trade (volume)	100	75	97
World trade (value)	100	54	77
World production:			
primary products	100	92	110
manufactures	100	70	120

17. For example, by W. A. Lewis, *Economic Survey, 1919–39*, 1949, pp. 59–61.

national economy because there was no general belief in, or desire for, such a system. This is reflected in the absence in the 1930s—in sharp contrast to the 1920s—of any serious international efforts to revive the system. Indeed, many countries discovered that the restraints they imposed on their external trade gave them more freedom than before to raise the internal level of activity.

As widespread and massive unemployment was the overriding problem for many countries the greater latitude over internal affairs was an important gain: it meant that expansionary movements at home were not necessarily halted or restrained by balance of payments consequences. In the context of the 1930s there was a general willingness to sacrifice some of the advantages of international trade if this allowed the internal level of unemployment to be more directly tackled. Against this background Britain's abandonment of the gold standard was therefore highly symbolic, but perhaps less practically damaging than might have been expected.

The development of new economic institutions

The de-stabilising effect of Britain's action on the international currency situation was, in any event, considerably softened by the operation of three important institutions. One of these was the Tripartite Monetary Agreement which was reached in 1936 when France[18] belatedly followed Britain (1931) and the United States (1933) by devaluing its currency. These three countries—with the aim of encouraging trade—agreed to manage their currencies in such a way as to stabilise the exchange rates between them.

The second institution was the sterling area, which emerged once Britain left the gold standard. It consisted of those countries which more or less tied the value of their currencies to sterling, finding it convenient to do so because Britain was their major market and London their reserve centre. Included in the sterling area was virtually the whole of the British Commonwealth (except Canada) plus a number of other countries (mainly in the Middle East, the Baltic, and Scandinavia). These countries pooled their international reserves

18. In the first half of the 1930s France was the centre of a small group of European countries—the gold bloc—which remained on the gold standard. The others were Switzerland, Belgium, and the Netherlands. The United States left the gold standard in 1933, but early in 1934 the price of gold in terms of dollars was again fixed, but at a level—$35 to an ounce—which confirmed the devaluation of the dollar.

in London and through their concerted strength contributed to a greater degree of international stability.

Stability was vastly enhanced, moreover, by the third institution, the Exchange Equilisation Account. The aim of this was to smooth out the variations in the foreign exchange value of the pound. After a difficult beginning in 1932, when its holdings of gold were inadequate to secure the essential control of the market, it was outstandingly successful, a technical triumph for the Bank of England. The essence of the operation was to buy sterling when the market—for reasons of speculation, seasonal change, or capital movements—was unloading it, and sell when the market was anxious—for similar generally non-trading reasons—to move into sterling. This, by keeping a reasonably constant value of sterling in relation to gold, provided something like the exchange stability function of the gold standard, but with two important advantages. There was not a formal, and almost irrevocable, commitment to a particular parity; and the movement of gold into and out of the country simply passed into and out of the Equalization Account without effecting any expansion or contraction of credit within the economy.

The operation of the Account thus secured some at least of the advantages of the gold standard system: in this sense it was the adoption of a general system of tariffs which marked for Britain a more decisive break with the past, the more especially because, with large and influential sections of the economy interested in their maintenance, they became virtually irreversible.

The gold standard abandoned: effects on Britain's internal economy

On the internal economy the influence of the abandonment of the gold standard was, potentially at least, almost entirely beneficial. Its major effect was to remove or reduce some of the pressures which had been acting on the domestic level of activity. Thus it became possible to reduce the rate of interest to encourage credit expansion once the overriding necessity to attract foreign short-term funds to maintain the parity of sterling had been removed. Similarly it became possible for the government to avoid cutting short a rising level of internal activity because it would lead to a worsening trade balance which encouraged speculation against sterling. These were possibilities that gave the government more latitude to pursue expansionary policies than was the case when the pound, especially an over-valued pound, was tied to gold. In the event, as will be argued later, the government took very little conscious advantage of them. Government policies thus made comparatively little direct contribution to the substantial upsurge in economic activity in Britain in the 1930s, whose first signs began to show themselves in late 1932.

Chapter 4

The Road to Recovery

British economic trends, 1932–37

Between 1932 and 1937 nearly all the key economic indicators for Britain moved confidently upwards.[1] There was then something of a recession in 1938, but this was very short-lived as expenditure for war gained momentum. To a substantial degree, of course, the revival of activity was simply the upswing of a trade cycle: 1932 marked, in terms of many economic indicators, the depth of a depression; 1937 was the peak of the recovery. The improvement in economic performance during the 1930s was, however, much more than just cyclical: even when comparisons are made with 1929—the peak year of the 1920s—1937 still shows a substantial improvement.

In most respects, but not in all. There were some important indicators which suggested that the British economic recovery of the 1930s was only partial. This was particularly marked where external trade was concerned.[2] It is true that, both in value (in current prices)

1. Some major economic indicators, 1929, 1932, and 1937 (Sources: Mitchell and Deane, *British Historical Statistics*, p. 272 and *Key Statistics, 1900–1966*):

	Gross domestic product (factor cost) £m. (1958 prices)	Industrial production 1924 = 100	Output per man–year (G.D.P.) 1958 = 100	Price index retail 1958 = 100	wholesale 1958 = 100
1929	12,233	113·3	78	39	37
1932	11,276	102·0	77	34	27
1937	13,926	147·7	84	36	35

2. British external trade, 1929, 1932, and 1937 (Source: *Key Statistics, 1900–1966*, pp. 14, 16):

	Value of imports £m.	exports	Volume of imports 1958 = 100	exports	Terms of trade 1958 = 100	Current balance of payments £m.
1929	1221	729	93	74	88	+103
1932	702	365	80	46	108	−51
1937	1028	521	96	59	97	−56

and volume terms, imports and exports had by 1937 considerably recovered from their 1932 levels: but exports in particular were still a long way below the levels of 1929 and, despite the rise in prices,

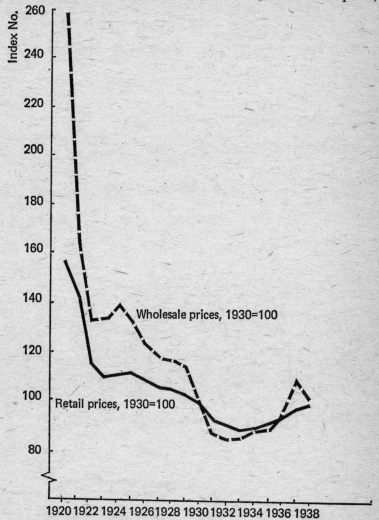

Figure 4.1 Indices of wholesale and retail prices, 1920–38.
Source: Based on Mitchell and Deane, *op cit.*, pp. 477–8.

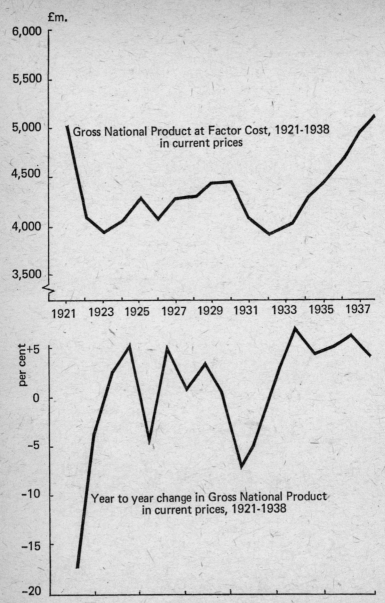

Figure 4.2 Gross National Product at factor cost, 1921–38, in current prices.
Source: *The British Economy: Key Statistics, 1900–1966.*

were still just below the level which had been reached in 1913. In 1937 the value of British imports was 83 per cent and of exports 71 per cent of their 1929 level: in volume terms imports just ex-

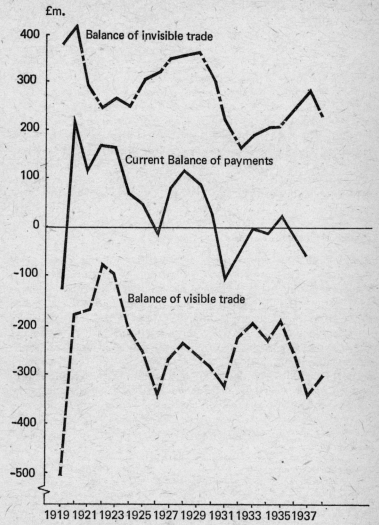

Figure 4.3 United Kingdom balance of payments, 1919–38.
Source: *The British Economy: Key Statistics, 1900–1966.*

ceeded, while exports were only four-fifths of, the 1929 level. Moreover, the current balance of payments which in the 1920s—while inadequate to maintain the substantial volume of long-term overseas investment and also provide adequate reserves—had normally been positive, became almost persistently adverse in the 1930s.

The trade deficit would, indeed, clearly have been even greater if the prices of imports—the volume of which was comparatively buoyant—had not fallen much more rapidly than those of the very sluggishly rising volume of exports. The slow growth of British exports was to a substantial degree a reflection of world trends; a marked feature of the 1930s was, as already noted, the extent to which the revival in world trade lagged behind that of world production. The universality of the basic trend does not, however, eliminate its concern for a major trading nation. No matter from what angle it is viewed, the external position was discouraging, and this must temper the more ebullient assessments of the economic achievements of the 1930s.

Unemployment

A second major source of reservation was the continuance of a level of unemployment which, for the upswing of a trade cycle, was exceptionally high. By 1937 unemployment was about half that of 1932 but it was still, both in absolute numbers and as a percentage of the insured working population, above that of 1929.[3] Despite some offsetting factors—the total number in civil work in 1937 was nearly two million (13 per cent) more than it had been in 1929—the overriding facts about employment in the 1930s were precisely the same as in the previous decade: at any particular time a significant proportion of the total labour force was unable to obtain work, and these unemployed were heavily concentrated in certain industries

3. Employment and unemployment in the U.K., 1929, 1932, and 1937 (Source: *Key Statistics, 1900–1966*):

	Number in civil work m.	Number unemployed U.K. 000s.	Percentage unemployed
1929	18·71	1,263	10·4
1932	17·96	2,829	22·1
1937	20·65	1,482	10·8

and certain regions of the country.[4] Indeed, the unemployment experience of the 1930s was persistently unfavourable even in comparison with the disappointing 1920s. The impact of this was eased by two broad factors. Firstly, the scale of financial assistance to the unemployed in Britain was, by general international comparison, relatively favourable; and secondly—and much more fortuitously—the generally downward drift in the cost of living enhanced the real value of these unemployment benefits.

These considerations eased the problem: they could not eradicate it. Despite, then as now, recurrent outbursts of well-shod indignation about idlers luxuriating on unemployment pay, for the vast body of people affected, unemployment was a deprivation in financial, social, and individual terms. This was generally recognised by all the main currents of political feeling. Indeed, Baldwin as early as 1923, during his first term as Conservative prime minister, had said in the speech announcing his conversion to protectionism: 'The fight against unemployment is vital. By its result the country would stand or fall. A man without employment is a man without hope or faith.'

The 1920s and the 1930s: a brief comparison

In terms of general economic growth, the 1930s seem to have been similar to the 1920s, or at least to the period from 1924 to 1929. The rate of growth of total output (about 2·2 per cent), total employment (1·3 per cent), and output per employee (0·9 per cent) was very much the same between 1924–29 and 1929–37. If the totals are broken down some differences emerge—output in manufactures and distribution grew faster in the 1930s, while construction and primary industries grew more slowly than in the 1920s. But the major point to notice is that the overall growth performance was broadly similar over most of the inter-war years, and that this growth performance compared favourably with the immediate pre-1913 experience, returning to something like the level achieved during the second half of the nineteenth century.[5]

1930s economically more favourable

However, despite these statistical and aggregative similarities between the 1920s and 1930s, there are still some cogent reasons for

4. The important regional aspects of unemployment will be more fully discussed later in this chapter. See below, pp. 111–14.
5. Dowie, *Econ. Hist. Rev.*, 1968, and Matthews, *Manch. Stats. Soc.*, 1964.

arguing that, for most of the people involved, the economic experience of the 1930s was more favourable. In part this was simply because the upward direction of the economy was more perceptible. Contemporaries seemed more conscious of improvement than they had been in the previous decade, although no doubt some of this consciousness was illusory and arose partly because the depth of the depression in 1932 had been so severe.

There seem also to have been greater steps made towards adjusting the industrial structure. This again was to some degree only psychological in that, as time went on, there was a greater degree of acceptance of the necessity for some sectors to decline. No doubt this consideration also helps to explain why industrial relations in the 1930s were comparatively placid, in sharp contrast to the massive and bitter strife of the 1920s.[6] Similarly, although the size and nature of the unemployment problem changed comparatively little—and then mainly for the worse—there was, with the flood of writing, research, and social heart-searching on the topic, a much greater awareness of the basically localised 'and structural nature of the unemployment problem.

Finally, there was no doubting the much improved performance of the British economy relative to that of most other industrial countries. In the general international upsurge of the years between 1925 and 1929 Britain had lagged markedly; but the British recovery which set in from 1932 was much more confident and perceptible than the faltering revivals in France and the United States (and although the same would not be true of Germany or the Soviet Union, few in Britain were prepared to accept the human costs which their expansions entailed). Most of these considerations had little effect on the real level of activity; but if the factors which seem to make the economic climate of the 1930s preferable to that of the 1920s are largely psychological, so too is the welfare that material and economic progress is meant to improve.

6. The massive unemployment of the early thirties might also have made the labour force more pliable. But although trade union strength—at least in numbers—fell in the early thirties, it then revived to a level above that reached before the general strike of 1926. Total trade union membership (in millions):

1925	1929	1930	1931	1932	1933	1934	1935	1936	1937	1938	1939
5·5	4·9	4·8	4·6	4·4	4·4	4·6	4·9	5·3	5·8	6·1	6·3

The influence of foreign trade

Many factors contributed towards the revival of economic activity in Britain from about 1932 onwards; but it is not easy to identify them all, and still more difficult to assess their relative significance. It has already been suggested that the abandonment of the gold standard, while relieving some constraining pressures, played a comparatively limited part. Much the same might be said about the second major aspect of government policy: the adoption of a system of tariffs. This was a fundamental change in British trading policy. For nearly a century, since 1846, Britain had been essentially a free trade country; in 1932 that position was decisively altered.

There are some suggestive parallels between 1932 and 1846, although the decisions they embodied pointed in opposite directions. Thus in both cases the change in policy had cast its shadow a long way ahead. The free trade cause was not victorious until 1846, but the battle went back to the publication of Adam Smith's *Wealth of Nations* in 1776, to Pitt's trade treaty with France in 1786, to Huskisson's reforms of the 1820s. Similarly, the abandonment of free trade in 1932 had been prefaced by the war-time McKenna duties imposed in 1915 and by the 1921 Safeguarding of Industries Act. The effects of these were to give substantial protection (a one-third *ad valorem* duty) to a small but important range of industries, including scientific instruments and motor manufactures. In addition there were a few more specific measures, such as the Dyestuffs (Import Regulation) Act of 1920 and the Cinematograph Films Act of 1927. This long slow swell towards protection was dramatically symbolised by the fact that the crucial Import Duties Bill was introduced in February 1932 by Neville Chamberlain, whose father's vigorous campaign for tariff protection had been decisively rejected at the polls in 1906.

Moreover, in both 1846 and 1932, the move was made as a direct response to an urgent crisis—the Irish famine in the one case and the breakdown of the international financial system in the other—by a government which had no specific mandate for such measures. But in both cases the change, when it came, was merely reflecting Britain's situation in the world economy. In 1846 British industrial supremacy was clearly established, and a policy of free trade was a useful means of exploiting this situation to her advantage; by 1932 it was equally clear that this supremacy had passed and that Britain's industry had at least as much need of protection as that of its rivals.

The influence of trade protection

The Conservative Party had for some time preached protection as a panacea. Baldwin, in 1929, pointing out the crucial nature of the problem of unemployment, had added that 'he was willing to fight it, but he could not fight it without weapons . . . and the only way to fight . . . was by protecting the home market'. This was still the Conservative stance when they entered, and dominated, the National Government in August 1931. The evidence, however, suggests that protection was a somewhat inept weapon. There is no indication that the British recovery of the 1930s resulted directly from the changes in trading policy. No doubt the adoption of a general tariff put some restraint upon the level of imports. Even so imports increased much more than exports—though this was partly because import prices fell more than export prices. Nor is there any clear sign that employment recovered first in the protected industries. The most expansive sectors for employment were distribution, professional and other services, and public utilities, sectors which were largely unaffected by tariff changes. It is true that without protection imports would have been still higher and employment in these protected industries lower, but the fact remains that the changes produced by the reversal of trade policy were inadequate to explain the buoyancy of the recovery.

There are, however, some mild indications that government trading policies changed the *pattern* of British trade. The imposition of a general tariff was, for example, a necessary prerequisite for the adoption of a policy of imperial preference: until Britain had a system of tariffs, she could not offer reduced levels to other Empire and Commonwealth countries. The Imperial Economic Conference which met in Ottawa in the summer of 1932 had, however, only very limited results. What emerged was largely a series of bilateral trading agreements between Britain and the various Dominions— later matched by other arrangements with the dependent colonies. These arrangements were quite similar to the series of bilateral agreements—about a score of them—that were negotiated with a succession of non-Empire countries during the 1930s. Each agreement, whether within the Empire or not, was the result of hard bargaining.

These agreements probably affected the channels of British trade to some degree—the proportion of British imports and exports from and to the Empire, for example, increased during the 1930s.[7] But this was trade-diversion rather than trade-creation.[8] That is, the net addition to total trade was limited: the export gains which Britain made in the Empire and treaty countries were substantially offset because they diverted competition into other markets where, in consequence, British goods found it even more difficult to maintain their position.

The terms of trade

In so far as recovery stemmed from trade at all, the major contribution came from a trend which was largely independent of government policy. The extremely favourable terms of trade for Britain, and manufacturing countries generally, in the 1930s, contributed to the economic recovery in two major ways, one negative and one positive. On the negative side, it meant that the strongly rising volume of British imports, compared to the much slower revival in exports, gave rise to a smaller deficit on current account than would otherwise have been the case. This was because the price of British imports was falling relative to the price of British exports, so that to obtain a given quantity of imports in 1937, the quantity of exports needed was 10 per cent less than it had been in 1929. Without this assistance, the trade deficits in the 1930s would certainly have been greater, and might have acted as a restraint on internal expansion. On the positive side, the continued decline in import prices, and especially of food, meant that real incomes tended to rise. This certainly contributed to the maintenance of consumer demand, which was an important factor encouraging economic activity in Britain in the 1930s.

It is possible to argue that Britain would have been better off if the terms of trade had been less favourable. At the basis of this

7. Percentage of U.K. trade with Empire, 1931 and 1937 (Source: S. Pollard, *The Development of the British Economy, 1914–50*, Edward Arnold, p. 198):

	% of U.K. imports from Empire	% of U.K. exports to Empire
1931	24·5	32·6
1937	37·3	39·7

8. See Katrak, *International Trade and the Balance of Payments*, Chapter 3. Trade diversion *can*, of course, result in extra trade: but this was not its major effect for Britain in the 1930s.

argument is the fact that higher prices for food and raw materials would have meant higher incomes for primary producing countries. This in turn would have meant a higher level of demand in these countries, and part of this would have been met from outside, and hence there would have been a greater demand for British exports. There is some plausibility in this, but the argument is greatly blunted because it concerns an entirely hypothetical situation. It was not an alternative which was open to Britain to choose. Given the facts of the situation, there can be little doubt that the highly favourable terms of trade for Britain contributed substantially to the vigour of the economy.

Cheap money

In considering the general impact of government policy on the economy during these years, it is important to realise that very few of the more significant measures were specifically directed towards increasing the level of activity. In so far as government policy did do so, the result was largely fortuitous. Tariffs, it is true, were largely justified on these grounds. But the more effective step of abandoning the gold standard and an over-valued pound was a crisis measure forced upon a reluctant government. And the still more effective step of moving towards lower interest rates was initiated primarily as a source of budgetary economy.

The word 'initiated' is in any event too forceful: in 1932 the market rate was already low and declining; the conversion in that year of the 5 per cent War Loan to a 3½ per cent stock took advantage of this trend to put a large and expensive part of the national debt (over one-quarter) on a cheaper footing. It represented a saving of over £30 million a year in government interest payments and it also represented a contribution by the wealthy to match those already imposed by Snowden's budget of September 1931—the first budget of the National Government—upon government employees and the unemployed.

But if the government's adoption of a cheap money policy started as a simple acceptance and exploitation of an existing situation, the passage of time brought a more positive adherence to cheap money. The abandonment of the gold standard had removed the need to keep interest rates up to attract foreign short-term capital, and the operation of the Exchange Equalisation Account largely insulated the economy from short-term external fluctuations. The authorities were thus able to keep Bank Rate at 2 per cent from June 1932 until 1939: they were prepared to do so not only because of the saving to government expenditure through lower debt charges but also because it was hoped that the low interest rates would stimulate investment and raise the general level of activity.

There is, however, not much evidence that they did do so: the total of new funds raised each year by non-government borrowers in the capital market in the 1930s was—although tending to rise after 1932—persistently below the 1929 level, nor is there any clear indication of credit expansion by the banks. But industrial investment in 1935 and 1936 was above that of 1929, and there are indications that firms relied more upon financing investment from their own resources. The strong probability is that the impact of cheap money on industrial investment was permissive rather than positive: that is, as business confidence improved, cheap money helped to ensure that any emerging investment plans were not deterred by high interest rates.

The housing boom

It is often argued that the housing boom provides a more direct connection between cheap money and economic recovery. The essence of the case is the assertion that it was the housing boom which was the driving force behind the economic expansion in Britain during the 1930s, and that the increased house-building derived from the existence of low interest rates.

Both parts of this assertion are open to challenge. The high level of activity in housing can only very partially be attributed to cheap money. It was at least as important that there was a strong underlying demand for new houses, although of course it was probable that cheap money—by lowering costs—encouraged the demand. Nor was the basic demand simply a function of the widespread existence of slums and much other old and sub-standard housing, although these factors did mean that there was an almost permanent latent need for more housing. At any particular time, however, something more is needed to transform this desire into an effective demand in the economic sense. In the 1930s several forces were working for such a transformation.

As will be seen later there was a very substantial shift in the location of industrial activity. The tendency, already evident in the 1920s and even earlier, for industrial development to centre upon London, the Midlands, and the South-east became more marked in the 1930s, and with it went a substantial migration of labour to these regions from Scotland, the North, and Wales.

Some indication of the direction and size of migration flows can be inferred from the table below.[9] The mere movement of population on this scale necessarily created a need and a demand for housing, but it was reinforced by two other major tendencies: improvements in transport and higher real wages.[10] The railways catered more extensively for a commuter traffic while the development of the motor bus and the spreading use of the motor car, and, much more marked, the bicycle, also encouraged a trend for people to live further from their work. The 1930s thus saw a considerable development of the habit of suburban living and this outward movement from town centres involved extensive new building.

To some degree the demand thus generated was given further substance by the rise in real incomes. This came from two main sources: from the favourable terms of trade by which British consumers gained from the fall in world agricultural prices; and from the fact that money wages, even in the most depressed years of 1929–32, fell much more slowly than prices.[11] Some part of the gains of higher real incomes was taken in the form of increased spending on housing either as rents or as mortgage repayments.

9. Increase in population, Great Britain and selected regions, 1921–37 (Source: *R.C. on Distribution of the Industrial Population*, H.M.S.O., 1940, pp. 22, 37):

	Nos. (000s)	%		Nos. (000s)	%
Great Britain	3,240	7·5	Mid-Scotland	99	4
London and home counties	1,803	18	Lancashire	44	1
Midlands	439	11	Glamorgan and Monmouthshire	−161	−9
West Riding, Notts., Derby	290	6	Northumberland and Durham	−31	−1

10. A. P. Becker, 'Housing in England and Wales during the Business Depression of the 1930s', *Econ. Hist. Rev.*, 1951.

11. Indices of wages and cost of living (1924 = 100), 1929–37 (Source: Mitchell and Deane, *British Historical Statistics*, p. 345):

Date	Money wage rates	Cost of living	Real wages
1929	98·6	94·9	104·0
1932	94·4	81·1	116·5
1937	103·1	91·0	113·5

These rising impulses on the demand side were further stimulated by sharp falls in building costs during the first half of the decade: the price of a small working-class house fell from £350 in 1931 to less than £300 in 1933, and costs continued to fall until 1935. At the same time, house purchase became markedly easier and cheaper to finance. There were funds available, partly because of the restricted domestic investment outlets, and even more because of the sharp deline in investment overseas. Moreover, the fall in building costs, combined with the usual stickiness of rents (which fell much less), and the absence of attractive alternative investment outlets made the providing of houses for rent a sensible investment during these years.

Cheap money also made a contribution here: it enabled a decline in mortgage rates which fell from 6 per cent to $4\frac{1}{2}$ per cent between 1932 and 1934. This significantly eased the size of the monthly or weekly repayments involved in house purchase and this was reinforced—and perhaps overshadowed—by the tendency of building societies to spread repayment over a longer period and to reduce the size of the initial payment.

All these developments were of the utmost significance especially since, unlike the 1920s when most new houses were either built by local authorities or received some state assistance, over three-quarters of the houses built in the 1930s were privately built and financed. None the less it is difficult to see that the prime source of the housing boom was the cheap money policy. Almost certainly of greater importance was the cumulative effect of the substantial migration of population, improved transport, higher real wages, lower costs in the industry, and the lack of attractive alternative investment outlets. Cheap money gave an extra stimulus to demand, but much of that demand would have existed anyway: cheap money facilitated the housing boom, but in itself did not cause it.

There is, in any event, some doubt that it was the level of activity in building which was the prime mover in the recovery from the economic depression. This is not to suggest that the scale of activity in house building has been called in question. In the nine years after March 1930 nearly $2\frac{3}{4}$ million houses were completed at an average rate in excess of 300,000 a year: this was a slightly higher rate than in the 1950s when competitive pledges by the two main political parties made housing something of a crusade. House building in the 1930s clearly involved a substantial scale of investment and this, with its multiplier effects, represented a useful contribution at a time when resources were generally under-employed. Its impact was, indeed, enhanced because in the first half of the decade, when idle resources were most evident, the number of houses completed was increasing each year, and hence provided an annual net addition to investment.

Perhaps even more important—since the industry is essentially labour-intensive—the increased building activity meant a direct increase in employment: between 1929 and 1937 the number of insured workers in building and contracting rose by over 350,000— nearly 40 per cent. If, therefore, the housing boom is not considered to be the main agent of the general revival of activity, this is not because its size and wide-ranging effects are themselves challenged, but because some still more significant cause can be identified. It has been strongly suggested that such a rival claimant can be seen in the growth of the so-called new industries.[12]

The new industries

The argument that the recovery in economic activity in Britain in the 1930s was closely associated with the growth of new industries and services has much plausibility. One might, for example, reasonably expect that newly-developing sectors of the economy would experience a relatively rapid rate of growth. Moreover, there is much to suggest that some of these new industries came into particular prominence during the 1930s. Certainly such products as motor vehicles, electricity, and artificial fibres were exerting a widespread social influence during this decade with the extending use of electrical appliances, motoring, and stockings and other clothes manufactured from artificial silk. And, finally, the fact that these industries and services depended largely on a relatively buoyant home demand—while the older staple industries were more affected by the depressed level of overseas demand—also suggests that their influence would be more expansionary.

Although the argument is plausible, however, it is far from conclusive. The importance of the contribution made by the new industries to recovery is far from easy to demonstrate or to test. In the first place there are formidable problems of definition. What is a 'new' industry? If all (or most) expanding sectors are implicitly defined as 'new', then it is not very surprising—and not very meaningful—to find that new industries are associated with growth. Again, if all new developments are classified as new industries—so that the

12. This case is fully argued in H. W. Richardson, *Economic Recovery in Britain, 1932–39*; 1967, pp. 82 ff.

very rapid expansion of department and chain stores is separated out from the general growth of retail distribution—then the possibilities of the residual old sectors expanding becomes highly constrained. In the second place, there are problems of measurement, since figures tend to be available only on a largely aggregative basis. It is thus difficult to delimit the contribution made by new industries to recovery.

Despite this, some indication of a fairly rough and ready kind can be given. Thus in five industrial sub-groups,[13] which would all fall pretty solidly within even a fairly restrictive definition of new industries, the numbers employed increased between 1929 and 1937 by over $\frac{1}{4}$ million, or nearly 50 per cent, as compared with a total increase in the number of insured workers of some 13 per cent. There are some indications, too, that the recovery in these industries came comparatively early—certainly before the end of 1932 when the first signs of recovery in the economy generally can be detected. It must be noted, however, that this hardly emerges from the employment figures: the number of insured workers in the same five industries in July 1932 was $8\frac{1}{2}$ per cent more than in 1929, compared to nearly 6 per cent for industry generally, while the unemployment rate in these industries in July 1932 was $18\frac{1}{2}$ per cent compared with nearly 23 per cent for all sectors.

But in terms of output and investment the depression was, in several of these industries, very mild indeed. The output of motor vehicles, for example, fell only 5 per cent from its 1929 peak and was already rising again by 1932; by 1933 output was 20 per cent above the 1929 level. Electricity supply continued to rise even between 1929 and 1932 and then expanded strongly, while the output of goods such as radios and refrigerators also moved upwards throughout the depression. And although net investment in the manufacturing sectors was negative in the three years 1931–33, it was still positive in such particular industries as motor vehicles, paper, and electrical engineering. Thus it is clear that the relative buoyancy in these new industries helped both to soften the impact of the general depression and to promote the recovery that followed. It is much less clear that this was a more important factor than housing.

13. The total number of insured persons in the following industries: electrical engineering; motor vehicles, cycles, and aircraft; electrical wiring and contracting; electric cables, wires, and lamps; silk and artificial silk, was:

July 1929	July 1932	July 1937
514 280	559,020	765,890

The impact of house building was both less ambiguous and of greater weight. In terms of output, employment, and investment it exhibited a marked recovery after 1930. Thus if attention is concentrated upon investment, with its crucial income-generating effects, the preponderance of housebuilding was especially marked. In the four main depression years from 1930 to 1933, houses accounted for one-third of the total gross domestic capital formation,[14] while the entire manufacturing sector—new and old industries—accounted for only one-seventh. In terms of net investment the disparity would be much greater.

The single major non-housing investment was for the provision of electricity supply. In particular investment on the provision of the National Grid, which had been started in the 1920s, was continued throughout the depression years. Indeed, it was, by a fortunate accident, at its peak between 1930 and 1932, when over £30 million was spent on this imaginative project.

Connections between housing boom and new industries

Perhaps the more important fact, however, is that house building and the development of new industries were often interrelated and mutually reinforcing in their effects. Part of the demand for housing arose, as we have seen, because of the changing pattern of industrial location. This was associated with the concentration of the new industries in the South and Midlands, and also with the way in which the use of electric power freed many sectors of industry from the northern and western pull of the coalfields, which had so dominated industrial location in the nineteenth century. At the same time the demand for houses also meant a strong complementary demand for electricity, electrical appliances, cars, and cycles.

14. Gross domestic capital formation, 1929–33 in £ million at 1930 prices Source: C. H. Feinstein, *Domestic Capital Formation in the United Kingdom, 1920–38*, C.U.P., pp. 38, 69, quoted in Richardson, *Economic Recovery*, p. 126):

	Gas, water, electricity	Transport and communications	Residential buildings	Manufacturing	Other	Total
1929	46	94	130	73	90	433
1930	52	87	122	68	106	435
1931	61	78	127	56	105	427
1932	58	50	128	54	82	372
1933	52	33	168	55	76	384

Moreover, in both sections—housing and new industries—the expansion, as already indicated, was partially dependent upon the growth in real incomes. As we have seen, real earnings for those in work rose continuously from 1929 to 1935. Indeed, in real terms (that is, allowing for the sharp fall in prices) total consumers' expenditure rose every year from 1929 onwards. This sustained level of consumption derived partly from the rising real incomes. As real incomes rose people naturally tended to spend at least part of their additional earnings, but this was reinforced by a complex set of economic and social causes. Of particular importance was the strong emergence of relatively new products—radios, vacuum cleaners, electric irons, motor cars—which induced people to spend, especially after the sharp drop in the prices of such goods in the early thirties.

The smaller family size also worked to free expenditure for products other than basic necessities, often leading to a substitution of demand for home-produced goods as against imported food. The decline in family size was a vital trend, and certainly one largely inexplicable solely in economic terms. But even if the reasons for this general movement towards limiting the family size are somewhat obscure, its broad economic results stand out sharply enough: they may be aptly suggested by the phrase that in the 1930s people preferred baby Austins to baby boys.

A number of different strands, then, contributed towards the maintenance of a high aggregate level of consumption. The overall result was that, even in the depressed years, there was a tendency for the total level of consumers' demand to rise. This, together with the investment it generated, was particularly vital, first in moderating, and then in reversing, the general economic downturn.

Government fiscal policy

The buoyancy of consumption, although basically accidental, was particularly fortunate because of the absence of any specific government action to maintain the level of demand. Crudely stated, the most widely-accepted view today is that in times of such severe economic depression the government should—among other things—run a budgetary deficit since this deficit would, either through additional government consumption, or investment, or both, generate increased aggregate demand and thus help to raise the general level of activity. The theoretical underpinning for this view was not, however, provided until the publication of Keynes's *General Theory* in 1936, and the orthodoxy of the early thirties was still that budgets should be balanced, preferably at a low level. There was much anxious struggle to bring this about: indeed, at an internal level, this was the essence of the British financial crises of 1930–31. In the event, despite—and partly because of—the alarums of the May Committee, there was a surplus of government income over government expenditure throughout the 1930s, except for the first full fiscal year of the National Government.[15] There was, to set against this, some increase in government borrowing—in the early thirties to finance the deficit in the unemployment fund, in the middle years to provide funds for the Exchange Equalisation Account, and at the end of the decade for rearmament.

Although orthodox balanced budget philosophy thus dominated practice in the thirties, it had become widely questioned. Indeed, strongly influenced by Keynes, the Liberal Party made a policy of large-scale expenditure on public works as a means of attacking unemployment a central part of its election campaign in 1929. Even the economists were by no means as unanimous and as slavish in their adherence to classical precepts as is commonly suggested. A group of five economists (Keynes, Pigou, Henderson, Robbins, and Stamp), asked to report to the prime minister on the problems of the economy in the autumn of 1930, showed a surprising willingness to modify classical precepts, and they explicitly rejected the Treasury view.[16]

However, such doubts had little effect. In general, government action continued to be directed by the view that increased public works would not assist the unemployment problem because they would simply lead to a corresponding reduction in private investment. Behind this assertion was an assumption that there was only a limited supply of savings and this was already fully utilised, so

15. Government gross income and expenditure in £ million, 1929–38 (Source: Mitchell and Deane, *British Historical Statistics*, pp. 395, 399):

	Income	Expenditure		Income	Expenditure
1929	836·4	760·5	1934	809·4	770·5
1930	815·0	781·7	1935	804·6	784·7
1931	857·8	814·2	1936	844·8	829·4
1932	851·5	818·6	1937	896·6	889·1
1933	827·0	833·0	1938	948·7	909·3

16. R. Skidelsky, *Politicians and the Slump*, 1967, pp. 202–15.

that if the government took up more there would be less available for the private sector.

The results of government policy

Government fiscal policy thus played little positive part in inducing economic recovery. Indeed, it might be expected on theoretical grounds that the cuts in expenditure and the increases in revenue imposed by, especially, Snowden's September budget in 1931 tended to worsen the situation. Looked at in isolation this would be true, but it is possible that the indirect effects of government fiscal policy offset, and perhaps even outweighed, its apparently deflationary impact. There was a general belief, especially among businessmen and foreign financiers, that a balanced budget was the proper policy. Thus, in so far as it increased the confidence of these groups, a restrictive budgetary policy might well have been basically expansionary in its effect.

The general verdict must, however, be that conscious government policy contributed little to recovery. The abandonment of the gold standard—which was hardly government policy—certainly removed some external pressures and the operation of the Exchange Equilisation Account constrained their later re-emergence. This was, however, basically negative: despite persistent current balance of payments deficits, the internal economic expansion of the 1930s was largely untroubled by the external situation. The adoption of protection was, indeed, meant to secure a more direct boost for the internal level of activity, but there is little evidence that much stimulus derived from this source. Rather more, probably, came from cheap money although, as mentioned earlier, the official motivation for encouraging lower interest rates was concerned with budgetary economy rather than with inducing extra investment. In any event cheap money was probably more permissive than causal: it removed a possible obstacle to recovery rather than directly promoted that recovery. Finally, budgetary policy, in its direct effects, was likely to have made matters worse although its ill-effects may possibly have been offset by its favourable psychological repercussions. The recovery stemmed much more from largely non-government sources: the buoyancy of consumption because of rising real incomes, the housing boom, and the emergence of areas of industrial expansion.

Late in the decade, in Britain as elsewhere, one aspect of government policy did have a positive and increasing effect on the level of activity in the economy. A reluctant but growing commitment to re-armament involved the government in a substantial expansion of expenditure from 1935 onwards. The extra activity thus generated certainly moderated the impact of the recession of 1938, and it was also reflected in such trends as the rise in steel output from less than 10 million tons in 1935 to over 13 million tons in 1939.

The changing industrial structure: growing industries

Perhaps the really significant feature of the economic upsurge of the 1930s—indeed, of the inter-war years as a whole—was that a considerable lurch forward was made in the adaptation of Britain's industrial structure. In its broad outline this movement was largely independent of government policies or even of particular economic events. Although the speed and timing were uncertain, it is largely beyond doubt that the relative importance in the economy of some of the nineteenth-century staple industries would decline from their pre-1914 levels. If anything, there was even more certainty that some of the new industries would show a powerful expansion. It is, for example, inconceivable that the demand for electricity should not have grown.

Electricity

Electricity emerged as an alternative to steam as a source of power for industry, and even though it was more expensive it still held strong advantages—greater cleanliness, convenience, and control— for many industries. Electricity was also preferable to gas as a source of lighting and virtually irreplacable for many of the products— telephones, radios, gramophones—for which there was a strong demand in the inter-war years. In the early years this demand was constrained, though by no means stifled, by the structure of the industry. There was a large number of small firms with very little standardisation. The construction of the National Grid and the setting up of the Central Electricity Board in 1926 radically changed this. The Grid enabled the Board to buy supplies from the most efficient producers and sell to local distributors; it was outstandingly success- ful and certainly contributed to the pace at which the demand for electricity grew in the 1930s. Electricity production grew more than six-fold from 4·3 million kilowatts in 1920 to 26·4 million kilowatts in 1939, and the essentially secular nature of the rising demand was clear from the fact that, apart from 1921, output grew every year regardless of the general state of trade.

Motor vehicles

The same secular trend, though less persistently strong, is seen in the output of motor vehicles which rose from 95,000 in 1923 to a pre-war peak of 526,000 in 1937. Government intervention in this industry was not as imaginatively constructive as in the electricity supply industry, and its total impact is difficult to judge. As part of the McKenna duties of 1915 an *ad valorem* levy of one-third was charged on imported cars, and this was retained throughout the inter-war years (and beyond). The protected home market presumably encouraged the growth of the domestic industry. On the other hand, the system of vehicle taxation favoured the less powerful cars which were less likely to sell in overseas markets, where the main demand at this time was for cars with a higher horse-power. It is also probable that the Road Traffic Acts of 1930 and 1933, largely aimed at protecting the railways from road competition, put some constraint on the output of commercial vehicles.

Much more important, however, were the structural changes within the industry itself. It was in the inter-war years that the industry came to be dominated by a few large firms. In 1913 the total output of 34,000 vehicles had been spread, though very unevenly, among nearly 200 producers: in 1929 the 182,000 cars (excluding commercial vehicles) were made by 31 firms, three of which—Morris, Austin, and Singer—contributed three-quarters of this total output. By 1939 there were effectively six main car producers (Nuffield, Austin, Ford, Vauxhall, Rootes, and Standard) who between them made 90 per cent of all cars. This was the unavoidable accompaniment of a strong trend towards mass production techniques which exerted a downward pressure on prices, although this pressure was, particularly in the 1930s, largely overridden by the production of a large number of models.

Aircraft, rayon, and other industries

There is a similar air of inevitability about the expansion of a few other sectors. The aircraft industry was clearly on a rising trend. However, before 1939 it had not developed a mass market: the total number of passengers carried abroad on all flights, British and foreign, was less than 10,000 in 1920 and reached just over 150,000 in 1937, but thirty years later it was 14·5 million.

Rayon, on the other hand, was an outstanding example of a new industry which had reached its mass market before 1939. Outside the chemists' laboratories, man-made fibres, until the Second World War, really meant rayon which was generally known as artificial silk. The industry was dominated throughout the inter-war years by two firms: Courtaulds, who had introduced rayon production to Britain in 1906, and British Celanese. Produced chemically from cellulose, the output rose from 5·5 million pounds of rayon filament or yarn in 1919, a little less than had been produced before the war, to 111 million pounds in 1939. Virtually no rayon staple fibre was produced until the late twenties, but by 1939 the British output was 58·5 million pounds. Strong as the growth was, however, it represented a substantial decline in Britain's relative position. In the 1920s Britain was still a leader in the industry—although American output (not surprisingly) surpassed that of Britain, the American industry was still largely dependent upon British technology and capital. In the next decade, however, the United States, Germany, and, especially, Japan substantially surpassed Britain in output, competitiveness, and technical progress.

No brief survey of the industries and products which were growing in importance in Britain between the wars could claim to be exhaustive. The industries mentioned above are simply a sample, though a fairly significant sample. There are, however, many omissions both major and minor. The chemical industry covers too large and variegated a range of products for it to be very satisfactorily described as an expanding sector. But parts of it were certainly growing with the development of new drugs, new processes and materials for cosmetics, and new products—such as plastics and synthetic rubber—to replace old naturally-produced materials or to meet previously unsatisfied wants.

The application of scientific discoveries in chemistry also contributed to the spread of photography, and to the emergence of new alloy steels which formed a highly expansionary sector of an industry which otherwise experienced considerable difficulty in these years. The examples might be extended—for example, by considering the growth of the radio industry or the introduction of high speed machine tools in engineering, but the general point is clear enough. The inter-war years witnessed a vigorous growth over a sufficiently wide range of industries (or parts of industries, or services) to produce a perceptible change in the overall structure of industry.

The changing industrial structure: declining industries

The new industrial balance which was achieved by 1939 derived at least as much from the stagnation or decline of some sectors of the economy as it did from the expansion of others. Fundamentally, the relatively declining sectors were responding to changes in demand. These were largely inescapable, but their effects were made worse—often much worse—by declining competitiveness on the supply side.

Coal-mining

In coal-mining, the industry most deeply affected, both these trends were very marked. The rate of growth of demand was substantially curbed by the emergence of substitutes (especially oil) and also by the much more economical use of coal (most of the growing use of electricity, apart from hydro-electric schemes, represented a more economical use of coal, and many of the technological developments in the steel industry worked in the same direction).

Before 1914 world coal consumption had been rising by some 4 per cent a year; in the inter-war years this fell to 0·3 per cent. The change was especially marked in world trade in coal, where total world imports actually declined by over 20 per cent between 1913 and 1937. Before 1914, moreover, the coal industry in many countries other than Britain was in a relatively early, though rapidly quickening, stage of development: in the inter-war years the degree of competition was much more intense. In addition, the strong inherent tendency of an extractive industry towards diminishing returns, declining productivity and rising costs was inadequately countered by technical developments. Only in the inter-war years, under most unfavourable conditions, was much headway made towards mechanisation.

The adjustment of the industry to all these changes, already made difficult by wartime expansion and the temporary post-war clamour of demand, was further complicated as both coalowners and colliers reinforced their existing reputations for intransigence. The attitudes had many sources—sociological, historical, and psychological—but they also had a sound economic basis: the coalowners faced with declining productivity, rising costs, stronger competition, and stagnant demand naturally looked for relief by attacking wages and hours (labour formed nearly two-thirds of the total costs); the miners equally naturally clung to their hard-won standards, especially as declining productivity already affected earnings for the dominant group of piece-rate workers.

Successive governments kept trying to look the other way—in vain, but their enforced interventions were mainly unhappy in their results. In the 1920s government action certainly did more to inflame than to calm industrial relations as could be seen, for example, in the failure to implement the findings of the Sankey Commission in 1919 as well as in the events leading to the General Strike of 1926 (above, pp. 30–4). The 1930 Act attempted to provide for the structural reorganisation of the industry that was always supposed to be the counterpart to the miners' accepting lower wages. However, the part of the Act which set up a Coal Mines Re-organisation Committee to encourage amalgamations was a dead letter: the owners seized only upon that part of the Act which provided for the control of output and prices. No doubt this contributed to the slightly rising trend of coal prices in the 1930s, and no doubt this in its turn encouraged some investment in the industry to increase the degree of mechanisation;[17] but, in a situation of massive unemployment in the industry, schemes to restrict output while at the same time increasing output per man had no appeal to the miners. There was, however, no generalised and open conflict in the industry in the thirties: after their batterings in the previous decade the miners' attitude in the 1930s was sullen and brooding.

It was in this atmosphere that the output of the industry fell from 267 million tons in 1924 to 257 million tons in 1929 and 231 million tons in 1939. It is important to note, however, that the extent to which the different coalfields were affected by these overall trends varies very widely. If, for example, attention is concentrated on the two largest areas—South Wales and South Yorkshire—there is a sharp contrast.

On the demand side, South Wales was especially dependent on the demand for steam-raising purposes and had always found its main outlets in the export market; South Yorkshire produced mainly manufacturing and household coal and looked almost entirely to the more stable domestic market. The relationship to the export market

---

17. Percentage of British coal output mechanically (i) cut and (ii) conveyed, 1921, 1933, and 1939 (Source: *Annual Reports of H.M. Chief Inspector of Mines*):

	(*i*)	(*ii*)
1921	14	n.a.
1933	42	30
1939	61	58

was particularly important since the total fall in output between 1913 and 1937 was only very slightly larger than the total fall in exports: the level of home consumption was little changed. On the supply side, South Wales was fully-developed before 1913 and had always been a high-cost area because of the disturbed nature of the seams; South Yorkshire was a still-developing coalfield with a relatively friendly geological structure that helped to keep costs down and profits up. Between 1913 and 1939 the output of coal in South Wales fell by over one-third: in South Yorkshire it rose by over one-fifth.

Cotton

The other major declining industries showed the same broad trends. The cotton industry was heavily dependent on export demand especially in underdeveloped countries, many of which were intent upon fostering their own textile industries. After the First World War India, as we have seen, produced more of her own cotton cloth thus undermining Lancashire's major pre-war market, while Japan also emerged as a formidable competitor. Cotton was also, particularly in the thirties, affected by the emergence of rayon as a significant substitute, as well as by the decline in demand for the finer cottons—Lancashire's specialism—caused by the general world depression.

On the supply side, the industry had long lagged in the adoption of technical changes—ring-spinning and the use of automatic looms were largely scorned in Lancashire before 1913, while financial difficulties made their adoption more difficult in the inter-war years. In any event, for most of the 1920s the belief was widespread—it received support from the Balfour Committee in 1928[18]—that Lancashire's troubles were largely temporary: this indeed was the basis for the general prevalence of organised short-time working. This—and the absence of structural reorganisation of the industry, which had been made more difficult by the substantial selling of mills at inflated prices during the brief post-war boom—tended to increase the level of costs at a time when demand was falling and foreign competition increasing.

18. The Committee on Industry and Trade was appointed by the short-lived Labour Government of 1924, and was under the chairmanship of Sir Arthur Balfour (later Lord Riverdale), a Sheffield steel manufacturer. Over the next five years it issued several reports on British industry and commerce dealing, as its terms of reference required, particularly with the export trade.

By the 1930s the permanency of the decline was recognised. One result was that the Lancashire Cotton Corporation, formed in 1929, pursued a slow and tortuous path of trying to concentrate production in a smaller number of more efficient mills. The negotiation of trade quotas, schemes for minimum prices and for the restraint of output dominated the decade. In 1936 the government also gave some help towards the removal of excess capacity, while just before the outbreak of war in 1939 the government was again called in to give statutory backing to an elaborate price-fixing scheme. Any judgment on these various expedients must bear in mind the enormity of the problem: in the short space of a couple of decades output had fallen from over 8 million square yards of piece-goods before 1914 to 6 million in 1924 and 4·3 million in 1937, the best year of the 1930s.

Shipbuilding

The decline in shipbuilding was even sharper. The industry had worked at high pressure through the war and the immediate postwar years when the rapid increase in freight rates encouraged a rush of new building. But the decline in general world trade after 1921, together with the vast increase in the world's shipbuilding capacity, made for an abrupt reversal of demand.

The industry had always been acutely susceptible to fluctuations in activity, but before 1914 the effects of these had been cushioned by the strong secular increase in world trade and hence in the demand for ships. Between the wars the situation was worsened by two tendencies: the fluctuations in economic activity were large in relation to past experience while there was only a sluggish growth in the total volume of world trade. Technical changes did help to soften these effects by making more tonnage obsolescent: the number of motor vessels, as opposed to steam ships, increased, and there was a growing demand for such specialised vessels as oil tankers.

On the supply side, a decline in Britain's relative share in world shipbuilding from its extraordinary pre-war dominance—British yards then built over 60 per cent of the world's new tonnage—was probably unavoidable. The war, however, acted as a forcing ground for new competition and, in the difficult years that followed, the excess capacity in British yards, compared with foreign shipyards, tended to be greater and their technical adequacy less, while several countries also gave direct subsidies to their shipbuilding industry. By 1937 Britain was building less than 40 per cent of world tonnage. The inter-war years thus saw the characteristic instability of the industry intensified and the impact of this was increased because there was also a declining secular trend in output.[19]

Agriculture

The postion in agriculture was somewhat different: it was, as it were, an old-established declining industry. Indeed, Britain's adoption of free trade made the decline of home agriculture more or less certain. The strongly complementary nature of international trade in the nineteenth century had meant that Britain could only sustain her steadily rising export of industrial goods by being prepared to accept primary products in return. The pace of agricultural decline varied substantially; it was slow until the 1870s when improvements in rail and sea transport greatly intensified foreign competition. Nor was the decline uniform. The depression of the 1870s and 1880s hit hardest at grain producers, since meat producers still gained for some time from the inadequacy of refrigerated shipping and from the rising home demand for meat as real incomes increased. But the trend was unmistakably downwards: despite a doubling of the total population, the numbers employed in agriculture fell from 2 million to 1·5 million between 1850 and the First World War.

The war brought a more general prosperity to agriculture and induced a new anxiety on the part of the government to expand agricultural output. Thus the requirements of war and of the immediate post-war shortages gave the impetus for the enactment of the Corn Production Act of 1917 (guaranteeing cereal prices for six years and laying down minimum wages) and the 1920 Agriculture Act (which again guaranteed prices for wheat and oats as well as regulating wages). But farmers did not have long to contemplate this newly proffered support to their industry. The 1920 Act was repealed in 1921 because the crash in world food prices would have required subsidies of an order of magnitude which clashed significantly with

19. Net tonnage of vessels built in the U.K. in thousands of tons, various dates, 1913–37 (Source: H.M.S.O., *Statistical Abstracts of the U.K.*):

1913	1,200	1929	931
1920	1,278	1933	84
1923	409	1937	453

the government's determination to pursue retrenchment and economy.

For the rest of the 1920s agriculture was left, as before 1914, to adjust itself as best it could to world competition. There were some exceptions: an Act of 1925 heavily subsidised the growing of sugar beet; agricultural land and buildings were, in 1928, exempted from rate charges; and in 1919 the Forestry Commission started to alter the aspect of some parts of the countryside. In general, however, agriculture received little effective government support in the 1920s.

This situation was sharply reversed in the following decade. No doubt this was partly because a particularly marked feature of the depression was the world-wide collapse of agricultural prices. More important, however, was the change in attitude, signified by the adoption of tariff protection for industry in 1932, since this change undermined the basic argument for *laissez faire* in agriculture; and, as the thirties progressed, the case for government assistance for agriculture was strengthened by the strategical demand arising from the growing threats of war.

There was thus a welter of government action. Most distinctive, perhaps, were the Agricultural Marketing Boards under which a variety of schemes for raising prices and restricting output were evolved. These Boards were set up under statutory powers: an ineffective Agricultural Marketing Act of 1931 was reinforced by a further Act of 1933, which added provisions for output control and, if necessary, tariff protection to the existing provision making any approved marketing scheme, accepted by two-thirds of the producers, compulsory for all. Probably the Milk Marketing Board set up in 1933 made the greatest public impact, although the Potato Board (1934) was probably the most, and the Bacon and Pig Board (1933) the least, effective.

In addition to the Boards, the Wheat Act of 1932 reintroduced a guaranteed price with a direct government subsidy, and a mainly ineffective restriction on output, while a number of agricultural products—especially meat—were given tariff protection. Other products were given quotas on imports from abroad besides, or instead of, tariffs. All this seems to have resulted in an increase in gross agricultural output, largely because of the continued rise in the relative importance of livestock farming at the expense of arable, and there was a continuation of the slow spread of mechanisation and more scientific methods. In most other respects, however, this burst of unco-ordinated government activity failed to reverse the general decline: the numbers engaged in agriculture fell; prices in the late thirties were still some 10 per cent below those of 1929; and much of the countryside still wore a look of neglect.

Other industries

The industries briefly described in this section by no means exhaust the declining sectors of the economy in the inter-war years. The numbers employed in the woollen industry, for example, fell and there was a similar decline in iron and steel, and pottery manufacture. Moreover, even in sectors which were generally expanding— like engineering—there were often contracting segments. The main point, however, is simply to establish that there were important sectors of the economy which were declining and that this process had a powerful impact on the overall structure of industry.

Besides the expansion of some relatively new industries and the stagnation of some of the older staples, a final trend affecting the balance of the economic structure was the expansion of local and service industries. Indeed, this was quantitatively the most important development. The trend itself was not really new, although some new occupations and services were involved—dry cleaning, for example. In general the provision of these services was a function of rising incomes and increasing industrial production.

The rising incomes left people with more resources after the satisfaction of basic needs, and hence stimulated the demand for improvements in public utilities, in distribution, and for a better provision of such services as education, medicine, and entertainment. The increasing industrial productivity released resources from manufacuring production to meet this diversified demand. This was a long secular process, but since total income and industrial productivity both rose in the inter-war years, it is not surprising to find that the professional and service sector of the economy was expanding more rapidly than industry generally, and hence contributing towards the general shift in the economic balance.

Overall results

Some indication of the broad outcome of these various influences can be obtained from studying the table below based on the industrial distribution of the insured population.[20] It is a very rough indicator. Figures based on the insured population tend to give too much weight to those occupations which are labour-intensive or have a low labour productivity, while under-stressing those which are capital intensive, or have a high labour productivity. Used with suitable caution, however, the table does give a reasonable indicator of the general direction and relative size of the changes that were taking place in the industrial structure.

Regional differences

It was of the utmost importance that these trends varied from industry to industry and place to place. It is obvious—indeed, it was the essence of the situation—that resources should be squeezed out of the declining and into the expanding sectors. But this process was made much more difficult and much more painful by two over-riding considerations: firstly, that shifts of this scale and pace had to be effected at a time of persistently heavy unemployment; and, secondly, that there was some tendency for the expanding industries to be concentrated in certain regions while the declining industries were heavily concentrated in others.

This perceptible shift in the geographical balance was a source of much concern and anxiety to contemporaries—just as its long continuance, even though in much more favourable circumstances, gives rise to intermittent unease in the present generation. The problem was carefully described and analysed by the Royal Commission on

20. Industrial distribution of the insured population, 1924 and 1937:

	No. in thousands	1924 % of total	No. in thousands	1937 % of total	1937 as % of 1924
Four declining industries*	2,348	20·1	1,673	12·2	71·3
Services and distribution†	2,841	24·4	4,375	31·9	154·0
Building and contracting	860	7·4	1,329	9·7	154·6
Six expanding industries‡	424	3·6	803	5·9	189·5

* Coal-mining; cotton; woollen and worsted manufacture; and shipbuilding.

† Distributive trades; commerce, banking, insurance, and finance; miscellaneous trades and services; tramway and bus services; and gas, water, and electricity supply.

‡ Electrical engineering; motor vehicles, cycles and aircraft; electric wiring and contracting; electric cable, apparatus, and lamps; silk spinning and artificial silk; scientific and photographic instruments.

the Distribution of the Industrial Population which was appointed in 1937 (and produced its report—the Barlow Report—in 1940) as well as in a non-government investigation on the location of industry published by Political and Economic Planning in 1939. In particular these studies highlighted the rapid expansion of London, the home counties, and the Midlands, in contrast to the relative decline of a group of regions, the definition of which shifted slightly for different purposes but which essentially consisted of Lancashire, the West Riding, Nottingham and Derbyshire, Northumberland and Durham, Monmouthshire and Glamorgan, and mid-Scotland. These declining regions could essentially be described as the older industrial areas. In aggregative terms this shift could be summarised as in the table below.[21]

Two points might be briefly added. These percentage changes might seem to be relatively small, but it needs to be remembered that the absolute numbers involved are very substantial—in 1937, for example, 1 per cent of the population meant nearly half a million persons. And the aggregates, as usual, conceal wide variations. Thus, although all the older industrial regions suffered a relative decline, it was only in Monmouthshire and Glamorgan that this also involved a fall in the absolute numbers of both the total population and the numbers of insured workers.[22]

Related to changes in industry

These geographical shifts were, as might be expected, closely linked to the changes that were taking place in the industrial structure. It is important, however, to understand the nature of this link. The new locational pattern did not really arise because, during the inter-war years, the expanding sectors moved out of the old industrial regions and into London and the Midlands. The Barlow Commission, in-

21. Percentage distribution of population and net output, 1924 and 1937:

	Total pop. 1924	Total pop. 1937	Insured pop. 1924	Insured pop. 1937	Net output 1924	Net output 1937
Relatively declining regions	37·9	35·9	45·9	40·8	49·6	37·6
London and Midlands	33·0	35·4	33·6	37·7	28·7	37·1
Rest of Britain	29·1	28·7	20·5	21·5	21·7	25·3

22. There are also variations of timing. Thus both Northumberland and Durham, and Lancashire showed an overall increase in the absolute numbers of total and insured population: but this was made up of an absolute rise in the 1920s and an absolute decline in the 1930s.

deed, found that for the most obviously expanding industries the rates of growth in the different regions between 1923 and 1937 were not widely dissimilar and, more significantly, that the growth rate for some of the older industrial regions surpassed that of London and the Midlands. All this meant, however, was that expanding industries —by and large—tended to expand wherever they were found. Thus one important feature of the link between the changing industrial structure and the changing geographical distribution was simply that the newer, more expansive industries were already largely concentrated in London and the Midlands by the early 1920s. In 1923 one-fifth of the insured population in London and one-quarter in the Midlands were engaged in the expanding industries; no other region had more than 10 per cent of its insured population in these rapidly expanding industries.

Even more important, however, was the extent to which, at the outset of these years, the relatively declining industries were concentrated in the relatively declining regions. In 1923 three-fifths of the insured population in Monmouthshire and Glamorgan were engaged in five declining industries; in Northumberland and Durham one-half; in Lancashire over one-third: but in the Midlands only 12 per cent were so employed and in London only 1 per cent.

A growing regional imbalance

The operation of these forces tended to be cumulative. Those regions with a heavy preponderance of stagnant industries found that this inheritance weighed down their future development. It meant that, with heavy unemployment and a growing atmosphere of neglect and dereliction, they became progressively less attractive for the location of new industrial ventures, especially since they provided a most unpromising local market. The Midlands and South were much less encumbered, and initially they strongly attracted the industries which were expanding because these industries were—often for largely fortuitous reasons—already partially concentrated in these areas.

Initially, for example, there were no very compelling economic reasons why motor-car production should have developed at Oxford and Coventry, but once established these centres then exercised a locational pull over the future growth of the industry. In addition the major factors determining industrial location were being radically modified. The nineteenth-century dominance of heavy industries and steam power had frequently made the availability of a railway and of coal the prime considerations. Both markedly declined in importance between the wars. The emergence of road transport made for much greater flexibility and efficiency in transportation, at the same time as changes were taking place in the industrial structure whereby the heavy industries, in which transport costs tend to be most significant, became relatively less significant. And the substitution of electricity or oil for coal as sources of heat and power greatly reduced the locational pull of the coalfields. With the decline in these factors the relative importance of the pull of markets increased, and this too contributed to the pull of London and the Midlands.

The two nations?

All these influences made for the emergence, in a very real sense, of two nations within Britain between the wars. These years, as we have seen, involved in the aggregate substantial increases in national output and productivity which were partly achieved by a significant shift in the balance of the industrial structure. In the regions south and east of a line drawn from the Humber to the Bristol Channel, the economic atmosphere was mainly conditioned by these expansive impulses: to the north and west of this line—in Wales, the North of England and Scotland—it was mainly conditioned by the diversion of resources away from the industries which had formed the backbone of the economic structures of these regions.

Looked at on a national basis, the inter-war years provide nice problems of judgment as to how far the strongly favourable economic trends—a healthy rate of growth, rising output per head, a strong level of demand—were offset by the more depressing aspects—particularly high unemployment and failing exports. But if the varying regional experience is taken into account some of these difficulties disappear or, at least, diminish. In an exaggerated and oversimplified way it could be said that the favourable trends were most evident in the southern part of the nation, while the unfavourable trends were concentrated in the north and west. In a very real way the overall verdict of contemporaries on the inter-war years was greatly conditioned by the part of the country in which they happened to be.

Unemployment differences

In no issue does this difference emerge more sharply than in that of unemployment. The incidence of unemployment varied on several counts. Not surprisingly it varied with age. The level of unemployment was higher for older men, although this was not because they were more likely to become unemployed but because, once they did lose their jobs, they found it harder to obtain new ones. Somewhat less obviously, the incidence of unemployment was disproportionately heavy in the age group from 18 to 24, workers in this age group being especially prominent among those who had been unemployed for a year or more. This seems to have been primarily caused by the practice—in an overstocked labour market—of firms taking on juniors who were then sacked as soon as they reached the age (usually either 18 or 21) at which they commanded the wages of an adult.

The chances of a man becoming unemployed also varied widely with the industry in which he happened to work. Over the decade from 1927 to 1936, for example, the average rate of unemployment for insured males ranged from 4·4 per cent in train and bus services to 40·8 per cent in shipbuilding. Even these dramatic differences tend, in some respects, to understate the real variation. In the first place, they take no account of the extent to which the total number of insured workers in an industry increased or decreased. Some industries had, for a variety of reasons, a relatively high rate of unemployment, and yet were obviously not depressed since they were expanding vigorously.

The real mark of a depressed industry was the coincidence of a high unemployment rate with a decline in the numbers engaged in the industry. Thus in coal-mining during this decade over 300,000 men (nearly one-third of the initial labour force) left the industry altogether, yet the average level of unemployment was almost 25 per cent. Secondly, they understate the real differences between industries because they give no indication of the period of time for which men were unemployed in the different industries. Some quite prosperous industries had high unemployment rates, but it was unemployment of a largely temporary nature. But in certain major industries—coal, shipbuilding, cotton—men, once they had lost their jobs, were unlikely to be re-employed for a long time.

Above all, there were the strong differences in regional incidence. Between 1929 and 1937 the average level of unemployment in the south-east was 9·1 per cent; in the north-east 20·7 per cent; in Wales 29·3 per cent. And once again these figures understate the position. Thus in Wales in 1937, the peak year of the recovery, the level of unemployment was over 20 per cent even though there had been a large outward migration of population. The discrepancy would, moreover, emerge still more sharply if smaller areas were taken. In Merthyr or Blaina or Brynmawr for several years in the early thirties seven out of every ten men were out of work. And in Jarrow, 'the town that was murdered',[23] six out of every ten men were unemployed in 1934, and over half of these had not worked for at least twelve months.

For, once again, the overall levels disguised the differences in the length of unemployment. In 1937, of those who were unemployed, less than one in ten in London and the south had been out of work for more than a year. In Wales, out of a much greater total, two out of every five had not had a job of any sort for over twelve months. For every long-unemployed man in the more prosperous areas there were seventy in the depressed areas.

In many ways it was the long-term unemployed who were the essence of the problem. In any general assessment of the economic conditions of these years it should be noted that large-scale, long-term unemployment—when many people able and willing to work none the less became more or less permanently unemployed—was a new phenomenon. It was, moreover, largely a phenomenon of the 1930s. In September 1929 only 53,000 out of the 1,150,000 unemployed—less than 5 per cent—had been out of work for over a year. By the summer of 1933 the number of long-term unemployed had leapt to nearly half a million.

Although the numbers then fall slowly to rather more than a quarter of a million in the autumn of 1937, there were at least two ominous features in this decline. In 1937 the long-term unemployed formed 27 per cent of the total number unemployed, which was higher than the 20 per cent of 1933 at the depth of the depression. In addition, during the recovery years of the mid-thirties, even the absolute numbers of the very long-term unemployed—that is people who had been continuously out of work for over five years—were increasing. In 1936 the number who had been unemployed for five years or more was greater than the number who had been unemployed for one year or more in 1929.

Overall effects of regional differences

Moreover, all these strands tended to come together. The industries which were hardest hit tended to be concentrated in the regions which

23. The phrase was the title of a book by the local Member of Parliament at the time. Ellen Wilkinson, *The Town that was Murdered: the life-story of Jarrow*, 1939.

were hardest hit. To be unemployed and over 55 was an especial misfortune; to be unemployed and a coal-miner was an especial misfortune; to be unemployed and live in South Wales was an especial misfortune. But to be an old, unemployed Welsh miner was an unmitigated disaster.

To some degree these regional disparities have spilled over into the present, but in a much softened form. Despite the general maintenance of full employment, the rates in some regions have been around double the national average: even so—apart from the special case of Northern Ireland—a regional rate as high as 5 per cent has been rare. Between the wars, however, the regional differences were both sharp and significant. Apart from the depth of the depression when all areas were severely, though still unevenly, affected, most of those living in the south had only a very limited experience of, and contact with, unemployment: but to live in Wales or the north, even for the relatively secure or wealthy, was to be constantly surrounded by the problems of a pervasive unemployment. Those in the south were thus most aware of the benefits of national economic growth: in the north it was the costs of national growth which were most in evidence. This sharply divergent experience tends to make any single overall verdict on the inter-war years misleading and perhaps even irrelevant.

Chapter 5

The British Economy since 1945: a Narrative Account

Plan of the chapter

The intention of this chapter is to provide a brief, mainly chrono-
logical, account of the development of the economy since the Second
World War. It begins, however, with an attempt to assess the main
economic changes which were induced by that conflict. The section
devoted to the six years of war is in no sense a narrative of that
period: the main concern is to draw attention to the major ways in
which the development of the economy after 1945 was conditioned
by the wartime experience.

The chapter ends with an indication of the regional variations in
economic activity in post-war years. But the main core of the chapter
is meant to provide a largely descriptive and narrative account of
the British economy since 1945. Part of the purpose of this approach
is to provide some of the essential background and factual information for the following chapter which attempts to explain and, to some
degree, to assess the course taken by the economy in this period.

The impact of the Second World War, 1939–45

The war began on 3 September 1939 and ended in 1945 (the war in
Europe ended with the German surrender in May, the Japanese
war continued until August). During its course the British economy
was more or less entirely transformed to a war footing. There was
a comparatively slow start to this process in the period (1939–mid
1940) of the so-called 'phoney war'. The transformation was, however, rapid in the next desperate year or so, when (until the German
invasion of the Soviet Union in June 1941 and the Japanese attack
on the United States naval base at Pearl Harbour in December)
Britain stood largely alone and greatly menaced. By 1943 the conversion of the British economy to total war was more or less complete. At that time $8\frac{1}{2}$ million people, nearly one-fifth of the entire
population, were mobilised in the armed forces or in the munitions

industries. Most of these (nearly 5 million) had been drawn away from industries and occupations which were now accorded a lower priority. Over a million had come from the formerly unemployed, but a vast number ($2\frac{1}{2}$ million) had been drawn from groups which were normally outside industry, especially housewives.

So great a diversion of resources achieved in so short a time naturally had large, and sometimes lasting, repercussions. Some of the most important of these sprang from the mechanism by which the transference was effected. There gradually emerged a formidable apparatus of planning directed towards assessing the resources available, discovering the various claims made on these resources, and deciding the allocations between these competing claims. Despite many shortcomings, there can be little doubt about the overall success of the system. The importance of this for the post-war economy was basically two-fold: it demonstrated that a substantial degree of government intervention was practical, and it built up a reasonably favourable attitude towards such intervention.

The system of control also had other lasting effects. For example, it was itself highly dependent upon information, and it thus gave a major impetus to the collection and processing of economic and social statistics—a small but strategic post-war growth industry. The wartime management of the economy also required some theoretical framework. Part of this was provided by the Keynesian economic theories which had developed in the 1930s. Central planning and control had to be concerned with the economy as a whole, and had to know which of the many variables to look at.

The new economics helped with both of these problems: it was cast in macroeconomic terms (i.e., it was concerned with broad aggregates—national income, the total level of demand and investment, etc.), and it directed attention to a few key variables. The use of the new techniques proved particularly useful in financial and fiscal policy, so that—despite the much greater stresses—inflation was more fully contained than in the First World War. The change was signalised by the publication, in 1941, of the first White Paper on National Income and Expenditure. In the post-war years this annual publication was highly important—especially as the wartime physical controls were gradually removed—and served as a cornerstone of the government's management of the economy.

The war also had significant effects on the industry of the country. There were numerous inventions and innovations—like jet engines and D.D.T. and nylon fabric—which were first introduced, or first adopted on a large scale, during the war. There were also significant shifts in the industrial structure. A whole range of industries catering mainly for civilian consumption—clothing, textiles, retail distribution, household ware—were sharply cut back during the war to free their manpower and other resources, but especially manpower, for war purposes. Most of the ill-effects of this were, however, made good fairly quickly after 1945—although the process entailed many difficulties, especially as there was an acute shortage of workers who were skilled in the specific specialisms of these industries. There were, in any case, important compensations. Thus the war demands acted as a positive stimulus to several industries—engineering and motor vehicles, aircraft and chemicals, steel and other metals—which had a strong peacetime potential.

The war and Britain's external position

Much more fundamental and much more damaging was the effect of the war on Britain's external position. There were several strands to this problem. In the first place, exports were substantially sacrificed to the needs of war. By 1945 only one in fifty of the British labour force was engaged in exports, compared to nearly one in ten in 1939.[1] Since imports continued to rise—especially with the need to obtain armaments from outside—and since there was also a large expenditure by British troops overseas, there was a serious and growing deficit on Britain's current balance of payments. A substantial part of this gap—some £5·4 billion—was met by grants from the United States and Canada. Despite this, however, Britain had to sell an important part of her overseas assets (worth about £1·2 billion) as well as running down her gold reserves.

This depletion of overseas assets and her gold reserves was the second main way in which the war weakened Britain's external position. The result was that Britain's income from invisible trade—in the form of interest and dividends on foreign capital—was substantially reduced, especially as the war had also involved heavy losses in British merchant shipping, another important contributor to overseas invisible earnings. Besides, a further method by which

1. In itself, however, this would not have constituted a major and permanent obstacle. For a few years after the war it was easy to export—though difficult to get the resources to produce goods for export—as demand was everywhere high, and Germany and Japan, two of Britain's major pre-war competitors, were temporarily out of the market.

Britain closed her wartime trading gap was simply by running up debts. Much of the expenditure by British troops abroad was met in this way, and particularly heavy indebtedness was incurred in India, Burma, and the Middle East. These debts totalled nearly £3·5 billion and formed the basis of the post-war sterling balances. Altogether, therefore, the basic effect of the war was substantially to increase Britain's overseas financial obligations while, in some important respects, simultaneously reducing her ability to meet these obligations.

The effect of the war on general attitudes

A less tangible influence of the war was the perceptible shift in attitudes which it induced. Social tensions were partly eased, largely because the Second World War, to a much more marked degree than the First, commanded general support and approval in the country. This broad agreement was reinforced by the shared experiences and hardships which were imposed by a war which, again far more than any previous conflict, closely and directly affected the entire population.

The coalition government under which the war was fought, once Winston Churchill replaced Neville Chamberlain as prime minister in May 1940, was a genuine expression of a national unity. The ready co-operation of the Labour Party in the conduct of the war also contributed towards another general change in attitude which accorded to the labour force as a whole more influence and concern. The source of labour's power was basically that it was in acutely short supply—from 1942 onwards indeed the Manpower Budget was the central instrument for planning the re-allocation of the nation's economic resources. The effect was to produce a climate of opinion favourably disposed towards ideas of social equity. Rationing ensured an equitable distribution of food and clothing; school meals were extended; orange juice, cod liver oil, and cheap milk were supplied for children and expectant mothers; and canteens were set up in factories.

Post-war reconstruction

The most forceful embodiment of this wartime attitude, however, was in the plans made for reconstruction after the war. In several fundamental ways the commitments arising from these plans vitally and pervasively coloured the entire post-war period. In terms of Britain's internal policies there were three main strands.

The first concerned employment. In May 1944 the coalition government in a White Paper on Employment Policy virtually pledged that the maintenance of a high and stable level of employment was in future to be a main aim of government policy. This commitment implicitly carried with it a general acceptance that governments *would* intervene, and *did* have responsibility for the level of activity in the economy—although there was still room for disagreement about how much responsibility and how it should be exercised.

The second main strand stemmed from the famous Beveridge Report.[2] This was a far-ranging document covering financial provisions for sickness, unemployment, maternity, old age, and burial. Proposals were also included for a health service and for the payment of family allowances. Benefits were to be available to all. Although altered in many details, the report, which met with an enormous popular response, served as the blue-print for the post-war Welfare State.

The last major strand centred on education, which was actually legislated for during the course of war in the Butler Education Act of 1944. The major provisions raised the school leaving age to 15 (put into effect in 1947) and provided free secondary education for all. The structure of state schooling in Britain was dominated by the Act until the late 1960s, when opposition to the existence of different types and levels of secondary education, which had grown up under the 1944 Act, gave rise to a powerful movement, supported by the Labour Party, for comprehensive secondary schools.

New international economic institutions

The war also saw a resurgence of the hope that the international economy, which had been so badly battered in the 1930s, would be restored and reformed. After long arguments and hard bargaining, the two major institutions were agreed to at a conference held in the United States (at Bretton Woods in New Hampshire) in July 1944. These were the International Monetary Fund (I.M.F.) and the International Bank for Reconstruction and Development (the World Bank). The basic purpose of the Fund was to attempt to re-establish stable relations between the currencies of different nations. The Bank was intended to be a source of long-term international loans to be

2. Sir William Beveridge, *Social Insurance and Allied Services*, 1942, Cmd. 6404.

provided for productive purposes and on a broadly commercial basis. In 1947 the General Agreement on Tariffs and Trade (G.A.T.T.) was also reached as a step towards reducing the level of tariffs and other trade barriers.

In 1945, the United States was overwhelmingly the dominant nation in the international economy. The war which had imposed strain and economic destruction in Europe had largely acted as a stimulant to the vast productive capacity of America. Thus it is not surprising that the I.M.F. and the Bank largely reflected the desires and interests of the United States. They seemed to be designed more to protect the interests of creditor countries than to solve the problems of debtor nations. The conditions of World Bank loans, for example, made them largely inaccessible to many of the nations who most needed them after the war. The Fund members subscribed $8·8 billion in gold and their own currencies and in return could buy from the Fund, by using their own currency, the foreign exchange needed to tide them over temporary balance of payments difficulties—but only to an amount proportional to their own contribution to the Fund. Members also had to agree to set parities for their own currencies, not to change these without consulting the Fund, and to work towards the relaxation of foreign exchange restrictions.

For some years after the war, however, the Fund was largely inoperative. The major source of many goods was the United States but nearly all nations lacked the dollars to pay for them. Such an acute scarcity of a single currency was far beyond the capacity of the Fund: in the event it was largely met by the generosity of American aid. All this, however, meant that only slowly were the conditions created which made it possible to move towards the system of freely convertible currencies and multilateral trading which had been envisaged at Bretton Woods.

General economic trends since the war

From the end of the war in 1945 until 1970, the time of writing, there was an almost continuous growth of real output and income. This is indicated in Figure 5.1. In the entire period from 1947 to 1970 there was only one occasion in which the real gross domestic product for a particular year was not greater than that for the preceding year. Even in that year—1958—the decline was less than 1 per cent. The post-1945 growth of the economy thus represented an improvement on the

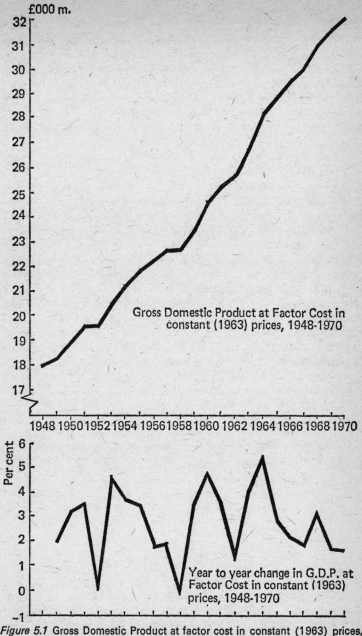

Figure 5.1 Gross Domestic Product at factor cost in constant (1963) prices, (1948–70). Source: *National Income and Expenditure*, 1971.

performance of the inter-war years, but in some respects the contrast with that period is less sharp than might be expected. After 1921 there were only two occasions up to 1938 when real gross domestic product fell—between 1925 and 1926 and for the two consecutive years of 1930 and 1931. But if the times of decline were then hardly more frequent than in the post-1947 period, they were a great deal more severe (real G.D.P. fell by about 6½ per cent from 1925 to 1926 and by nearly 8 per cent from 1929 to 1931).

The really marked contrast between the economic trends of the inter-war years and those of the post-1947 period emerges when unemployment figures are examined. The fluctuations in economic activity between the wars were taking place at a level which was well below the economy's full employment potential. The United Kingdom unemployment rate was persistently above 10 per cent, and frequently well above that level. After 1945 there was a remarkable transformation: for the next quarter of a century up to 1970 the annual unemployment rate for the United Kingdom remained below 3 per cent, with the single exception of 1947, when it was 3·1 per cent.[3] It was, moreover, usually well below this level—for fifteen of these twenty-five years the rate of unemployment was less than 2 per cent. There was some slight tendency for the level of unemployment to increase over time—certainly the average rate was higher during the 1960s than it had been in the previous decade—but the dominant feature was the way in which unemployment was restricted to an exceptionally low level for an extremely long time.

An inflationary trend

Partly as a result, both wage rates and earnings moved upwards.[4] Figure 5.2, however, indicates that a substantial part of the higher

3. United Kingdom unemployment rates, 1946–69:

1946	2·5	1952	2·1	1958	2·2	1964	1·7	1970	2·7
1947	3·1	1953	1·8	1959	2·3	1965	1·5		
1948	1·8	1954	1·3	1960	1·7	1966	1·6		
1949	1·6	1955	1·1	1961	1·8	1967	2·5		
1950	1·5	1956	1·2	1962	2·1	1968	2·5		
1951	1·2	1957	1·4	1963	2·6	1969	2·5		

4. Wage rates refer to the minimum, or standard, rates of wages which have been agreed within an industry. Earnings more nearly reflect actual gross pay, which may differ from the standard wage rate because of the operation of a large number of factors, such as overtime working, local allowances, premiums above the standard rate given in particular districts or within individual firms, etc.

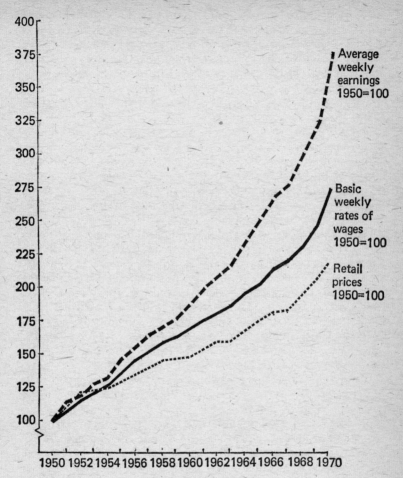

Figure 5.2 Indices of earnings, wage rates, and retail earnings, 1950–70.

Source: Department of Employment and Productivity, *Statistics on Incomes, Prices, Employment and Productivity*, June 1969 and the *Employment and Productivity Gazette*, September 1971.

money incomes were simpy absorbed by rising prices. The price increases indicate another feature which is largely peculiar to recent times, that of a pronounced and prolonged inflationary trend. At all events if attention is confined to the 150 or so years since the end of the Napoleonic Wars in 1815, the period—starting about 1940—of three decades of continuously rising prices is unique. Indeed, it is possible—the evidence is somewhat elusive—that on balance the century before 1913 was one of slightly declining prices and, after the rapid war-induced increases from 1914 to 1920, the inter-war years also saw an overall decline.

The modern inflationary trend was not, it must be noted, confined to Britain but was part of a widespread experience. Certainly a more or less continuous rise in prices was a feature common to all the major industrial nations. Attempts to make international comparisons of price changes encounter many statistical and conceptual pitfalls, but the evidence (at least for the decade after 1956) suggests that in some countries—like France and Italy—prices rose faster than in Britain, while in others—the United States and, less noticeably, Germany—prices rose more slowly.

Despite this comforting generality of the inflationary experience and the cosiness of Britain's apparent comparative moderation, the rising price trend has from time to time aroused considerable anxiety. There are several reasons for this. For example, it is argued that the price mechanism works less efficiently in times of inflation because rising prices tend to produce accounting profits in all activities, and hence discourage the re-allocation of resources from unsuccessful to more successful lines. There was also an underlying fear that the inflationary process might get out of control and develop into a situation of hyper-inflation.

Perhaps, however, there were two particularly pressing and substantial causes of anxiety. In the first place, inflation tended to redistribute income, often in ways—such as at the expense of old-age pensioners—which were considered undesirable. And secondly, because inflation was thought to have adverse consequences for the balance of payments, especially if British export prices were rising faster than those of some of her major competitors. The persistent precariousness of Britain's post-war balance of payments situation, and the way in which the external position often became a factor dominating internal economic policies, made this aspect of inflation of particular relevance.

The external balance

The major trends in Britain's post-war balance of payments are indicated in Table 5.1 and Figure 5.3. They reveal that normally—

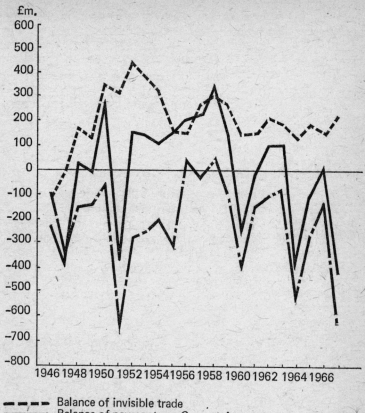

£m.

Balance of invisible trade
Balance of payments on Current Account
Balance of visible trade

Figure 5.3   United Kingdom balance of payments, 1946–67.

Source: H.M.S.O., *United Kingdom Balance of Payments*, 1968.

the exceptions were 1956, 1958 and 1970—there was a deficit on visible trade. Such a deficit has, however, existed for at least a century and, in itself, was not a matter for anxiety. Before 1914, however, the deficit on visible trade was almost invariably turned into a surplus on the current balance of payments by large net earnings on invisible trade—interest from overseas investment, insurance, banking, shipping, and similar services. The overall sur-

Table 5.1 U.K. Balance of Payments Summary, 1946 and 1950–70 in £millions

	1950	1951	1952	1953	1954	1955	1956	1957
Imports (f.o.b.)	2312	3424	3048	2927	2989	3386	3324	3538
Exports and re-exports (f.o.b.)	2261	2735	2769	2683	2785	3073	3377	3509
Visible balance	−51	−689	−279	−244	−204	−313	+53	−29
Invisible balance	+358	+320	+442	+389	+321	+158	+155	+262
Current balance	+307	−369	+163	+145	+117	+155	+208	+233
Balance of long-term capital				−134	−194	−191	−122	−187	−106
Balance of current long-term capital transactions				+29	−49	−74	−277	+21	+127

Source: *United Kingdom Balance of Payments*, 1968 and 1971.

plus on current account was then normally re-invested overseas making for a net outflow of long-term capital from Britain.

In the 1950s the surplus on invisible earnings was still sufficient—except for 1951—to outweigh the deficit on visible trade: but in the 1960s it was normally insufficient for this purpose, with the result that the current balance of payments was usually unfavourable. This was not without its effects on the pace of economic growth during these years.

Economic growth

In general the economy grew at a faster rate during the post-war years than had previously been the case. Between 1948 and 1968 real gross domestic product increased at an average annual rate of 2·7 per cent, compared with 2·2 per cent between 1922 and 1938—and this also compared well with Britain's economic growth before 1913.[5] The improvement over past performance would seem to be a source for modest satisfaction, but it has been completely overshadowed by a different kind of comparison.

Towards the end of the 1950s it became fashionable to construct tables comparing the growth rates of different countries. From these, as Table 5.2 indicates, the United Kingdom emerged as a comparative laggard, a situation which persisted during the 1960s. This slower rate of economic growth in Britain as compared with other major industrial countries has, indeed, become the central issue of concern over the performance of the economy. This is hardly surprising, especially as it seems to be a phenomenon that has only emerged

5. Based on *The British Economy, Key Statistics 1900–66* and D. C. Paige, F. T. Blackaby, and S. Freund, 'Economic Growth: the last hundred years', *National Institute Economic Review*, July 1961.

1958	1959	1960	1961	1962	1963	1964	1965	1966	1967	1968	1969	1970
3377	3639	4138	4043	4095	4362	5005	5054	5255	5674	6916	7202	7882
3406	3522	3732	3891	3993	4282	4486	4817	5812	5122	6273	7061	7885
+29	−117	−406	−152	−102	−80	−519	−237	−73	−552	−643	−141	+3
+315	+260	+151	+158	+224	+204	+143	+185	+156	+254	+355	+581	+576
+344	+143	−255	+6	+122	+124	−376	−52	+83	−298	+288	+440	+579
−196	+255	−192	+68	−130	−196	−372	−215	−119	−153	−143	−92	−191
+148	−121	+299	−25	−8	−72	−748	−267	−36	−451	−431	+348	+388

since 1950: before that time the rate of growth of the British economy seems to have been broadly comparable to that of other similar countries.[6]

Table 5.2   **Annual average percentage rates of growth**

	G.D.P., 1950–60
Belgium	2·9
France	4·4
Germany	7·6
Italy	5·9
Sweden	3·3
United Kingdom	2·6
United States	3·2

Source: A. Maddison, *Economic Growth in the West*, Allen & Unwin, 1964.

Re-adjustment to peace

Compared with 1918, the celebrations at the end of the war in 1945 were relatively muted, and so were the expectations for the future. In place of the extravagant hopes of 1918, there was at the close of the Second World War a mood of wary optimism. Certainly there was no delusion that somehow the wastes of war had made possible an instant affluence; still less was there any belief that a major economic advance could be based on resources extracted from the defeated and exhausted enemies. In 1919, too, there had been a widespread nostalgia for the pre-war world and its economic mechanisms at home and abroad: in 1945 there was little tendency to look back

6. Maddison, *Economic Growth in the West*, p. 28.

on the systems and institutions of the inter-war years as embodying any such kind of mythical golden age. In Britain it was in this atmosphere and this mood that a Labour Government under Clement Attlee was returned to office in the election of 1945—a Labour Government, moreover, which for the first time commanded an overall parliamentary majority.

In contrast to 1919, when the government had procrastinated until the pressures for social action had subsided or had been subdued, Attlee's administration was more than ready to set the pace itself. The government introduced, for example, a series of nationalisation measures. The first of these provided for the nationalisation of the Bank of England. In many respects this was merely a symbolic act since the Bank had long ceased to act in a private profit-making capacity.[7]

In the years after 1945, moreover, the Bank continued to exercise a good deal of independence, to advocate openly its own policy lines, and occasionally to criticise publicly the policies of the government. There is some difference of opinion on this matter, but the most general view is that the exercise of its independent judgment by the Bank is probably both healthy and desirable. The possible disadvantages have, in any event, been largely modified over the years by the evolution of closer links between the Treasury and the Bank, and by the gradual acceptance by the Bank that, ultimately, overall financial policy must be laid down by the Chancellor.

The nationalisation of the coal industry was even more of a foregone conclusion. The industry had been a political, as well as an industrial, battleground for a generation; the miners had long and persistently advocated a solution of state ownership; and the newly-elected Labour Government was fully committed to their support. Vesting date—when control of the industry passed to the nine members of the National Coal Board—was 1 January 1947 and took place to the accompaniment of much celebration in the colliery districts. Exactly a year later the British Transport Commission took over for the nation the railways, road haulage services, canals, and docks. Air transport had already been dealt with in 1946 when

7. It was, however, a symbolism which was highly charged with significance for many in the Labour movement—and outside—who believed that the Bank had played an unfriendly, if not sinister, role in the crisis of 1931. The Act did, however, make it quite explicit that the Chancellor could, if it were deemed necessary in the public interest, issue directives to the Bank. This ultimate ministerial control did not make much immediate difference in practice.

British European Airways Corporation was set up to match the British Overseas Airways Corporation which had been taken under national control in 1940. In addition the generation and distribution of electrical power was vested in a central authority in 1948, and the gas industry was taken over, though on a more decentralised basis, in 1949. Finally, the iron and steel industry was nationalised by an Act of 1949 under which the vesting date was in February 1951.

Most of these changes, with various alterations in the details of organisation, have survived; although much of the road transport industry was returned to the private sector in 1953, and the iron and steel industry was to be a bone of political contention for the next two decades. The extension of the public sector of industry was thus both substantial and permanent: nationalisation was the major method of securing industrial reconstruction during the immediate post-war years.

In addition to nationalisation measures, however, the post-war Labour Government was also active with more general social legislation. This may be illustrated by brief reference to three of the most dominant examples. Housing was made a major priority; the National Insurance Act of 1946 brought into a single unified fund the provisions for unemployment, sickness, and pensions; and the National Health Service was brought into operation in July 1948.

Loans from the U.S. and Canada

All these changes were brought about against an economic background that was highly unpromising. Britain had by 1944 concentrated her economy upon the needs of war to an extent unmatched by ally or foe,[8] and the relaxation of this as the end of the conflict loomed into sight was relatively gradual. This single-mindedness was made possible only by an extensive dependence on lend–lease aid from the United States. Under this Britain was from 1941 onwards able to secure supplies from the United States without having to pay for them in dollars or exports.

This important prop for the British economy was, however, removed much sooner than had been expected. Allied planning had proceeded on the basis that the war in the Far East would last eighteen months to two years after the end of the struggle in Europe: in the event the atom bomb narrowed this gap to three months. The un-

8. W. K. Hancock and M. M. Gowing, *The British War Economy*, 1949, pp. 365 ff.

foreseen abruptness of this ending of the war against Japan brought an immediate, and immensely disruptive, halt to the flow of American assistance to Britain. Lord Keynes was instantly despatched to the United States to negotiate some stop-gap dollar credits. The effective amount of the loan was $3,750 million at 2 per cent interest to be repaid over 50 years, the first repayment being delayed for five years to allow Britain to readjust her economy to the needs of peace. In addition, Canada also extended a loan of $1,250 million to Britain.

The Americans had acted less generously than had been hoped. Not that the financial terms of the loan, especially for so desperate a borrower, could be called harsh; but there was a widespread feeling that a loan was not the most appropriate remedy for Britain's economic vulnerability, which arose directly out of the extent of Britain's commitment to the war. Moreover, although the financial terms were mild, the loan involved a major political exaction— the immediate ratification by Britain of the Bretton Woods Agreement which was concerned with the post-war operation of international trade and finance.

Britain had been closely involved in the discussions leading up to the Bretton Woods Agreement and accepted the general principles which it embodied: none the less the American insistence on ratification by Britain as part of the loan negotiations was hotly resented for two main reasons. It seemed that the Americans were exploiting for political purposes the financial plight to which Britain had been reduced by her efforts in a common cause; and also some parts of the Bretton Woods arrangements—calling for rapid trade liberalisation and early convertibility of sterling—seemed highly inappropriate to Britain's immediate needs.

The loans were avowedly stop-gap measures, but nobody had foreseen just how short a gap the credits would be adequate to bridge. The American loan became available in July 1946: just over twelve months later it was rapidly approaching exhaustion. Three main trends contributed towards this disastrous drain. The first, and least important, was simply bad luck. The unusually severe weather in the winter of 1947, at a time when coal was acutely short, caused industrial disruption on a major scale. Closed factories and disorganised transport services involved a substantial loss of exports at a crucial time.

The second, and much more significant, source of outflow arose because Britain was importing—especially from North America— far more than she could pay for in goods and services. The loan was being used to bridge the gap between the shortfall in exports and the bloated level of imports. In 1947 it quickly became clear, however, that the hopes that the dollar loan would be able to perform the same service for at least a further two years were not going to be realised.

The third, and final, drain upon these resources came when, as had been agreed, Britain reluctantly made sterling convertible. The Americans had insisted on making their loan conditional upon Britain agreeing to sterling convertibility. Their hope was that this would hasten the return to an international economy less encumbered with trading and foreign exchange restrictions. The British plea that convertibility in 1947 was premature was viewed with suspicion in the United States, where Britain was regarded as a formidable trading rival, and was perhaps thought to be using American loans to build up a strong reserve position.

In hindsight at least—the British case seems overwhelming. The war had, as we have seen, greatly weakened Britain's balance of payments situation, while it had also led to a reduction of overseas capital assets, an accumulation of external liabilities and a decline in the gold reserve. In face of such weakness a policy of convertibility could only hope for success if there was in fact a widespread willingness and desire on the part of foreigners to hold sterling. There was, however, no real prospect that they would do so, especially as there was a world-wide shortage of dollars. In 1947 the United States was the only country able to supply many of the goods which were in short supply in the rest of the world, and hence everyone was anxious to obtain the dollars with which to buy the goods.

Moreover, it is important to realise that the move towards convertibility was a unilateral action on the part of Britain—though not one which would have been taken voluntarily—and thus sterling was made convertible at a time when nearly all other currencies, apart from the dollar, were not. Consequently foreign holders of sterling earned in current transactions could convert these pounds into other currencies—which almost always meant into dollars—at the official rate. They promptly did so on a large scale. The result was a one-way traffic which, with Britain's limited reserves of gold and dollars, could not be long sustained: in less than five weeks the 'dash for convertibility' had been abandoned. The only purpose served was to demonstrate to the Americans that their expectations of a rapid return to settled trading conditions were wildly optimistic;

and the demonstration was an expensive one for Britain, since in the process the credits which had been intended to ease the transition of the economy to a peacetime basis were exhausted.

The economic crisis of 1947

The outflow of dollars thus provoked a serious economic crisis for Britain in the summer and autumn of 1947. Thus it was the external situation which—setting the pattern for the next two decades or so— was at the basis of the crisis. The high level of internal demand, however, also contributed to the difficulties since some part of this expressed itself as a demand for imported goods or as a demand for goods which might otherwise have been exported.

Yet another factor contributing to the crisis was the hesitant nature of the government's response as the difficulties mounted. There had been, as we have seen, unusually severe weather in the first half of 1947: the government, however, delayed recognition of the resultant fuel crisis until the breakdown was imminent. Even more important, the government delayed the suspension of sterling convertibility even though it was immediately clear that the adoption of this course was leading to an enormous outflow of reserves.

The crisis provoked an autumn budget to curtail consumption— such emergency budgets were to become another recurring symbol of economic crisis over the following decades. Even before the budget the crisis had led the government to attempt (by the Control of Engagement Order of July 1947) to operate a peacetime direction of labour. In addition there was an extension of import controls. Thus the crisis induced a temporary reversal of the trend towards reducing reliance upon direct controls as a means of managing the economy.

Much more significantly, the crisis of 1947 marked an important turning-point in the assessment of the economic problems facing Britain. Until this time there was a widespread feeling that, once the pent-up wartime demand had been worked off, the major problem would be one of countering deflation. At the close of the war there had been a widely-held expectation that a slump—analogous to that of 1921—was approaching. The 1947 crisis, the crisis of an economy clearly operating at a high level of demand, helped to accelerate acceptance of the fact that the problem of curtailing inflationary pressure was likely to be a much more permanent issue than had been foreseen at the end of the war.

1947–51

The trend towards rising prices and higher wages emerged still more clearly in the ensuing years—domestic prices increased by about 40 per cent between 1945 and 1951—and produced a marked shift in government policy. There was greater realisation that the main-tenance of full employment, which continued to command general acceptance, tended to exert an inflationary pressure. Moreover, inflation in Britain—or at least a greater rate of inflation in Britain than in other countries—increased the problems of the external balance: for (if the exchange rate was fixed) inflation tended to in-crease the price of British goods relative to those of competing countries. Full employment and the maintenance of a high level of activity remained major objectives, but government policy was also directed towards limiting the inflationary effects of such aims.

The shift towards disinflation as a major aim of policy was initiated by the first post-war Chancellor of the Exchequer, Hugh Dalton, in his autumn budget of November 1947, the budget which also induced him to resign because of a minor budget leak. The policy of disin-flation, aiming to hold down the level of internal demand, was carried on with a kind of moral fervour by his successor at the Treasury, Sir Stafford Cripps; and the change of direction also led eventually to a reappraisal of the cheap money policy.

Cheap money

Cheap money—the persistence of a low rate of interest—had begun, as we have seen, in the 1930s. Although its initiation in 1932 had been the result of market forces rather than of deliberate policy, it soon came to seem attractive in itself. In particular, low interest rates were thought to stimulate the level of activity in the economy by encouraging investment. In the under-employed economy of the 1930s, this was certainly a desirable end—though we have already cast some doubt upon the effectiveness of cheap money in this respect (above pp. 88–9)—but in the already fully-employed post-war economy its relevance was less obvious. In particular, the pursuit of cheap money clearly made it impossible for a government to use monetary policy (the raising of interest rates) as a means of restrain-ing the level of demand.

None the less Hugh Dalton was strongly attached to the idea of cheap money and made its pursuit central to his policy. With hindsight, he has been consistently attacked for this adherence to an expansionary measure at a time of inflationary pressure. This was, it is argued, simply adding fuel to the flames. There is certainly some substance to the charge. There is no doubt that Dalton expended an excessive amount of energy in his attempts from 1945 to 1947 to drive down the long-term interest rate to $2\frac{1}{2}$ per cent. None the less, in the context of the time, the case for cheap money was much more persuasive than it came to appear during the long era of rising interest rates which followed.

Low interest rates had continued unbroken since 1932, including the war years with their high level of activity, and had come to assume an orthodoxy of their own. Moreover, the expectation of impending depression made it seem prudent to maintain such a useful weapon against this danger. There was also much to be said for financing some of the basic and unavoidable reconstruction needs as cheaply as possible. The government had, for example, issued large amounts of stock as compensation to the private owners of undertakings which had been nationalised: it seemed sensible to keep down the cost of interest payments on such stock.

As time went by these arguments dwindled in cogency, but it is quite misleading—though understandable because of Dalton's enthusiasm—to suggest that the cheap money policy represented the will of a single man or even of a single party: for some time after the end of the war it commanded a general adherence. Indeed, Dalton's departure in 1947 by no means marked the decisive abandonment of the cheap money policy. Certainly, Cripps made little use of monetary policy in his attempts to keep the level of internal demand within bounds. The imposition of a high interest rate might have cut down the level of investment, but Cripps preferred to place reliance upon fiscal (budgetary) policy to keep down the level of demand by maintaining high tax rates.

Although there were no attempts to drive down the level of the rate of interest, which showed a gentle rise—of about 1 per cent—over the next three years, there was no decisive abandonment of the cheap money policy by the Labour Government. It was, however, becoming increasingly difficult to ignore monetary policy, especially as the armoury of direct controls was progressively dismantled. These controls—especially building licences, the allocation of scarce materials, and the government's fairly direct influence over the substantial volume of public investment—were felt by many (including Cripps) to render interest rate policy largely irrelevant.

Controls in general were progressively relaxed after 1947, the so-called 'bonfire' of controls in November 1948 being followed by a similar relaxation in 1950. The trend towards de-control certainly affected the ability to exercise a direct restraint upon investment. None the less it must be noted that the controls necessary for influencing investment were the slowest to go: in particular, restraints were maintained over capital issues; and building licensing—though relaxed—was not removed until 1954. Moreover, the Korean War (starting in June 1950) enforced for a time a stiffening of the process for allocating scarce materials.

External deficits and Marshall Aid

The changes that were made after 1947—the persistent budgetary pursuit of disinflation and the gentle relaxation of a cheap money policy—certainly contributed towards the reduction of inflationary pressure by 1950. They were, moreover, strongly supplemented by the remarkable success of the appeals—which from Cripps sounded like moral imperatives—for voluntary restraints. The average level of wages, for example, rose only by 5 per cent between February 1948 and the autumn of 1950, despite the more rapid rise (8 per cent) in the general level of retail prices.[9]

Restraint, budget surpluses, and dearer money were, however, inadequate to solve the external problem, especially in the short run. There seemed to be no escape from substantial external deficits—particularly with the United States—if quite minimal levels of output, consumption, and investment were to be maintained. And any substantial or rapid recovery seemed, in its immediate effects, likely to increase these deficits. Moreover, this was true not only of Britain but of Europe generally. There was in the immediate post-war years —and indeed, through most of the 1950s—a world-wide dollar shortage. It was this critical situation that American aid magnanimously solved, or at least vastly eased.

The offer of aid from the United States to Europe generally was embodied in a speech made by the American Secretary of State, General George Marshall, at Harvard University in June 1947. The offer was made conditional on Europe undertaking some degree of economic co-operation. There was an immediate and enthusiastic response in Europe: Britain joined with France in issuing invitations

9. J. C. R. Dow, *The Management of the British Economy, 1945–60*, 1964, p. 35.

to a European economic conference which eventually led to the establishment of the Organisation for European Economic Co-operation (O.E.E.C.) in April 1948. In the same month the United States Congress approved the Foreign Assistance Act. By the end of 1949 Marshall Aid had provided Europe with some $7 billion, and the assistance played a vital part in restoring production and facilitating the emergence of a greater degree of currency stability in Europe.

Britain received assistance under the Marshall Plan until 1950. Even so Britain's external position remained threatening. Each country receiving aid had been required, in 1948, to produce a plan indicating how reliance on this 'extraordinary assistance' was to be removed over the course of the next four years. The British document had emphasised the need to restrain consumption to allow resources to be diverted to investment and exports, and to hold down the level of imports. The external deficit would thus be progressively decreased. During 1948 this seemed to be achieved; but the first half of 1949 saw the dollar gap widening once again, mainly because the United States economy was experiencing its first post-war recession. This was fortunately mild, but the resultant reductions in American imports were still great enough to unsettle Britain's precarious external position.

Britain's gold and dollar reserves were, moreover, considerably affected by her role as banker for the sterling area. The American recession meant an especially sharp curtailment of raw material imports from Commonwealth countries and these, like Britain herself, were slow to react by imposing import restrictions on goods from the United States. This added force to an already existing underswell of speculation against sterling, which many held to be overvalued in relation to the dollar. In September 1949, in conditions of mounting exchange crisis, sterling was devalued by 30 per cent. Except for this final act, the whole process of sterling crisis was to be frequently repeated in the years which followed.

The 1949 devaluation

There was at the time, and has been since, much debate as to whether the extent of the 1949 devaluation was excessive. The case in favour ran largely in psychological terms: that a large devaluation would end the speculation against sterling. The case against rested on the argument that a greater devaluation than seemed necessary simply on the grounds of prices and costs would mean that the British terms of trade were made worse than they needed to be. Britain would therefore have to export more in order to achieve a given volume of imports, and the wisdom of this was particularly questioned because exports were still limited as much by shortage of supplies as by high prices. Indeed, the point was made—both at the time and since—that an upward revaluation might have been more appropriate since at this time there was no real difficulty in selling exports. Germany and Japan had still not, in 1949, re-emerged as major competitors, and there was still a general world-wide shortage of supplies.

More important was the timing of the 1949 devaluation. There was a widespread conviction, both at home and abroad, that a devaluation in the external value of the pound was bound to have come some time: but the fact that it was adopted under duress and at a time of acute crisis had at least two important repercussions. It made the operation much more expensive because it came at the end of a long period of speculation against sterling, during which the authorities had had to buy sterling at the high official rate, thus draining away the currency reserves. And it appeared as a failure of government policy which was thus largely discredited. Perhaps it is unrealistic to expect governments to take such traumatic steps when things are going well: at all events the same process was, to some extent, repeated in 1967.

After the devaluation of 1949 there followed a period—to the last quarter of 1950—when the reserves were increased from their depleted levels, although how much of the increase was the direct result of devaluation, and how much of it arose from the 'wage-freeze' imposed by Sir Stafford Cripps and from the strong revival in activity in the United States, is difficult to know. The latter influence, together with a general rise in world industrial output, did push up commodity prices strongly. This meant that, because of their sales to the United States, the dollar reserves of the Commonwealth countries rose: but the rise in commodity prices also meant that Britiain's own terms of trade deteriorated sharply. Both factors were intensified by the outbreak of the Korean War in June 1950.

The economic crisis of 1951

These trends gradually produced fresh strains in the economy, and the strains were sharply compounded by the decision to undertake a substantial expansion in defence expenditure.[10] This meant not

10. In 1949 defence expenditure had been about £750 million: by December 1950 the estimate was for £4,700 million to be spent during the 3 years 1951–53.

only that a rising proportion of national output was to be ear-
marked for defence—difficult enough in an already full-employed
economy—but that the armaments demand fell especially heavily on
the engineering and building industries, thus competing directly
with exports and investment. Defence needs also required extra
imports of raw materials and machine tools. And all this at a time
when—and these were the more immediate causes of strain—the
terms of trade had moved sharply against Britain; when rising import
prices were adding irresistibly to the head of steam, which had been
building up during the years of voluntary restraint, pressing for wage
increases; when the dollar imports of the rest of the sterling area
were high because of the bloated level of their earnings from commodity sales; and when the Persian seizure of the oil refineries at
Abadan in March 1951 led to a sharp fall (of about £150 million)
in Britain's invisible earnings. It is arguable that the budget of
1951—Hugh Gaitskell's first and last—might have eased some of the
pressure by cutting back consumption still more than it did; but it is
difficult to avoid the conclusion that in the general climate of 1951
economic strain was largely unavoidable.

In the autumn of 1951 the strong outflow of reserves carried the
Labour Government with it and there was ushered in a long period
of Conservative administration. But although the dollar deficit
reached its peak in October, at the end of which month the new
government took office, the causes of the crisis had by then begun
to wane—although the crisis itself, and the loss of reserves, continued
until mid-1952. Commodity prices had indeed already passed their
peak by mid-1951, and this was particularly important because the
rise of import prices was alone sufficient to account for all of the
deterioration in Britain's balance of payments in 1951. A number of
controls, particularly over raw materials, had been reintroduced.
Moreover, the new government immediately put into effect extra
import controls which had been prepared by their predecessors, and
added still further import restrictions at the beginning of 1952.

After the yawning deficit of 1951 the balance of payments was in
respectable surplus in the following year. This could not be attributed to any rise in exports, which fell in volume and showed only
a modest increase in value. The value of imports, however, fell
markedly. Three factors contributed to this: import prices declined;
the tightening of import controls restricted the volume of imports;
and a decline in industrial output made for a reduced demand for
raw materials. It was only to the last of these influences that the

government's new emphasis on monetary policy made any substantial contribution,[11] though this explicit reinstatement of monetary policy was significant in its own right.

The 1950s

Monetary policy was more actively used after 1951 and provided an important additional means of controlling the economy. The major reliance, however, continued to be placed upon fiscal policy. Moreover, the Conservative administration, which started a long period of office in 1951, continued to pursue most of the same broad objectives of economic policy as had the previous Labour governments. This, indeed, led to the economic policies of the decade being dubbed as 'Butskellism', a word compounded from the names of the first post-war Tory Chancellor (Butler) and the last Labour Chancellor (Gaitskell) to imply their essential sameness of outlook. Thus after 1951 full employment was still a major priority; there was a general acceptance of the social services; and de-nationalisation did not extend beyond steel and road transport. Nor did the new government appreciably accelerate the sedate pace set by their predecessors for the removal of direct controls.

There was only one brief break in this underlying continuity. This came in the second half of 1957 when the Chancellor, Thorneycroft, intended to make a 'sound' currency the overriding, or at least the prime, objective of economic policy, and to leave the level of employment as a secondary objective. This potential, and significant, shift in emphasis was, however, never put into practice: in January 1958 the Chancellor resigned because the government marginally overshot his determination to keep government expenditure constant, and the two junior Treasury ministers—Nigel Birch and Enoch Powell— went with him.

The most fundamental reason for the basic similarity since 1945 in the approach of all governments to issues of economic policy is so obvious that it is easy to overlook. These governments, in contrast to those of the inter-war years, all accepted the proposition that a major function of government *was* to control the economy. In addition all British governments in this period have been faced with a more or less continuous series of economic crises. These—especially as they have mainly emanated from Britain's precarious external

11. For a different view see A. J. Youngson, *The British Economy, 1920–57*, 1960, pp. 175–6.

position—have placed serious constraints on government action. The resultant economic management has mainly taken the form of adjusting the budget, supplemented by *ad hoc* packages of monetary changes, to influence—especially—the total level of demand.

A minor by-product is that any attempt to describe the impact of this major influence upon the economy tends to lurch forward disjointedly from year to year, and budget to budget. This is all the more marked because throughout these years it proved impossible to steer a steady course—or, at all events, fairly sharp changes in direction were made which were said to be unavoidable.

Government budgetary policies

These discontinuities in the direction taken by economic policy were not immediately apparent. The general tone of economic policy from 1952 to 1955 was persistently expansionist. At the time of the 1952 budget the economy was nearing the end of the external crisis and was threatening to slide into internal recession. But the indicators available failed to reveal this, and the general climate of opinion was that the still precarious external situation required a further cut-back in home consumption.

In this atmosphere Butler's 'wait and see' budget of 1952 was considered to be optimistic. By the following year, the healthy balance of payments position encouraged positive action to stimulate a sluggish upward trend in production: the budget of 1953 was thus sharply expansionary, with cuts in income tax and purchase tax and the granting of investment allowances. The influence of the budget was, moreover, reinforced by a strong housing drive as Macmillan, the Minister of Housing, energetically discharged the Tory election pledge to build 300,000 houses a year.

However, expansion seemed to be threatened towards the end of 1953 by a decline in production in the United States. But in the budget of 1954, constructed in the shadow of what appeared to be a gathering American recession, Butler boldly refused to cut back the level of activity in Britain as an advance precaution against the effects of this possible recession. In the event, the decline in activity in the United States was largely offset by a remarkable increase in European production, which both maintained world commodity prices and sustained a rise in the level of world trade. Hence Britain's expansionary trend—which itself contributed to this European upsurge—was able to continue largely unabated.

The expansion, however, overreached itself in 1955 when it was given a further, and massive, stimulus by the pre-election budget of 1955. This was a major error. Unemployment was very low (1·1 per cent), the pressure of demand was clearly strong and rising, the level of investment was responding vigorously to the incentives given in the two previous budgets, and the domestic boom was sucking in imports on a scale sufficient to turn the external balance into deficit. These were not the conditions in which to give consumers another £135 million of spending power: but this was what was done by the 1955 budget. No doubt this budgetary bounty was partly influenced by the impending general election, but there was also a widespread impression—especially in the Treasury and the Bank of England—that monetary policy could effectively curb any excesses. Indeed, there was an erroneous but fashionable tendency to attribute the economic expansion since 1952 almost entirely to monetary policy, and hence to attribute to it extensive powers of control.

These delusions were rudely shattered in the summer of 1955. As early as February—well before the expansionary budget—some mild monetary warning signals had been hoisted; in July these were greatly intensified with a squeeze on bank advances, cuts in the investment plans of nationalised industries, and tightened hire-purchase regulations. Even so, a run on the currency reserves—which largely derived from the high level of home demand but was also fed by rumours that sterling was to be made fully convertible—enforced an autumn budget.

A long period of restraint followed, lasting until the middle of 1958. This fairly prolonged and fairly persistent attempt by the government to keep down the pressure of demand arose initially from the need to curb the external drain on reserves caused primarily by the high imports induced by the boom of 1955. The measures already taken in 1955 (the credit restrictions of July and the autumn budget) were continued and reinforced in 1956. There was a further package of credit restrictions in February when Bank Rate was raised 1 per cent to 5½ per cent, hire purchase regulations were further tightened, and cuts were made in public investment. Macmillan, who had succeeded Butler as Chancellor in December 1955, followed these with a mildly deflationary budget. These restrictions might, however, have been soon eased if it had not been for two other events which had sharp repercussions on British economic policy: the Suez adventure at the end of 1956, and the heavy currency speculation in the early autumn of 1957.

Suez and the economic crisis of 1957

For Britain, the main economic effect of the abortive invasion of Suez—apart from enforcing a temporary re-imposition of petrol rationing—was to set off intensive speculation against sterling. The loss of currency reserves may, indeed, have been one factor in the rapid termination of the military operation. Arrangements were made for Britain to draw reserves from her quota in the International Monetary Fund and these were supplemented by the negotiation of additional rights to draw currency from both the I.M.F. and from the United States. These measures seemed to be fully sufficient to contain the situation but Thorneycroft, who had become Chancellor when Macmillan became Prime Minister in January 1957, made only slight relaxations in his budget, and he continued to maintain the currency restrictions.

Despite this caution, and despite a favourable current balance of payments, a major currency crisis emerged during August and September. The crisis was largely caused by external factors. The franc was *de facto* devalued in August and there was much speculation as to the possibility of other adjustments following, the two most important and likely of which seemed to be a revaluation of the mark and a depreciation of the pound. The uncertainty led to a substantial loss of reserves and required a strong package of restrictions to lend credence to government insistence on maintaining the value of the pound. Bank Rate was raised to 7 per cent, which then seemed sensational and had a significant psychological impact; the banks were asked to place a ceiling on advances; and public expenditure was to be held firmly in check.

As has been already mentioned, all these measures—when coupled with the altered tone and content of accompanying ministerial pronouncements—indicated a new emphasis in policy towards giving control over inflation some degree of priority over maintaining unemployment at the very low levels which had become customary since 1945. It was the implicit rejection by the Cabinet of this altered emphasis which led to the resignation of Thorneycroft, Birch, and Powell in January 1958.

The general atmosphere of restraint survived their departure but it was no longer an issue of doctrine. Thus, although Heathcoat Amory's first budget of 1958 gave no encouragement to expansion, the continued favourable trends in the balance of payments, coupled with declining industrial production and rising unemployment, gradually induced a change. In the course of a slow relaxation during the second half of the year, the restraints on bank advances, public investment, and hire-purchase were removed. This moderate stimulus was vastly augmented in the budget which preceded the election of 1959. The extensive tax reductions and the re-introduction of investment allowances turned a faltering recovery into a mounting boom.

The 1960s

Something of the same pattern of bursts of expansion being followed by periods of restraint, the so-called stop–go progression of the economy, continued into the 1960s. In some crucial respects, however, the similarity was only superficial. In particular the underlying balance of payments situation had deteriorated markedly. In the 1950s there had been a favourable current balance in every year except 1951 and 1955: in the 1960s there was normally an unfavourable balance. The aggregate current balance surplus for the decade of the 1950s was well over £1,000 million: for the 1960s this had been converted into an aggregate deficit of nearly £500 million.

As a result the constraints imposed upon the management of the economy were substantially increased, especially as successive governments eschewed devaluation as a remedy, or at least as a respite. In particular, any attempts to stimulate the level of activity in Britain —since they necessarily led to an increase in imports and tended to discourage exports—were likely to set off speculative moves against sterling. One by-product of this was that more attention was paid to new and altered methods of economic control, such as planning, incomes policy, and the use of more sensitive economic regulators, such as special deposits.[12] But the most pressing and persistent effect of the deterioration in the balance of payments was to make the British economy even more vulnerable to any external pressures.

The sterling crisis of 1961 made this abundantly clear. The rapid expansion generated in 1959 led to a very considerable increase in imports in 1960, when the current balance swung from a surplus of about £140 million in 1959 to a massive deficit of over £260 million

12. Special deposits are deposits which the clearing banks are obliged, when required, to place with the Bank of England. These funds then cease to form part of the liquid assets of the commercial banks thus, it was thought, making it more difficult for them to grant extra credit to their customers. This additional weapon of monetary policy was first exercised in April 1960 but was never very effective. For fuller treatment see Peters, *Private and Public Finance* (Chapter 6) in this series.

in 1960. Although the budget of that year was largely neutral, it was soon followed by restraining measures. In April hire-purchase restrictions were imposed and, for the first time, the commercial banks were required to make special deposits with the Bank of England, which had the effect of reducing the ability of the banks to extend credit. In June these special deposit requirements were increased and Bank Rate was raised to 6 per cent. These measures were by 1961 already curbing internal demand and correcting the current external balance, which moved into surplus from mid-1961.

The effect of the revaluation of the German mark in March 1961 overrode such favourable trends. There was a strong belief that a sterling devaluation would follow, a belief which led to an outflow of British currency reserves. To meet this, the already declining internal trends were given a further strong downward push by the stern measures introduced by Selwyn Lloyd in July 1961, after his mild first budget a few months earlier. Bank Rate was lifted to 7 per cent, government expenditure curbed, bank advances squeezed, a pay pause introduced, purchase tax raised—and both the Bank of England and the Treasury would have favoured still fiercer cuts. Since the internal level of activity was slowing down, the acute sensitivity of the economy to external pressures was clearly demonstrated.

The overall restraint was maintained in the budget of 1962, although by then the chief danger was economic recession rather than excessive demand. This error, arising largely from a misinterpretation of the economic signals by the Treasury officials, no doubt played some part in Macmillan's abrupt dismissal of Selwyn Lloyd in July 1962 when Maudling was appointed Chancellor. Even so, economic restraints were only slowly eased during the second half of 1962, and the winter of 1962–3 saw a marked increase in unemployment.

It was in this atmosphere that the budget of 1963 offered substantial tax reliefs to inject more spending power into the economy. The resultant expansion was much stronger than expected and a mild attempt was made to dampen down the pace of growth in the 1964 budget. The attempt was, however, largely ineffective and the rising level of home activity was leading to high imports and a mounting current balance of payments deficit. But in the months following the budget, the months running up to the general election, no significant steps were taken to control these trends.

In part, the absence of control represented an experiment to see whether, in place of the—by now habitual—stop–go techniques, the economy could be allowed to pursue a path of steady growth. Balance of payments difficulties were bound to emerge—at least for a time—(as the sustained activity at home led to higher imports) but these would have to be dealt with in other ways. The most obvious methods were through the use of some kind of import restrictions (by direct controls or by the imposition of a surcharge) and/or by devaluation. As it turned out, the size of the overall deficit (on current and capital account) in 1964 was approaching £800 million, much larger than had been envisaged. With so great a deficit it is reasonably certain that the internal growth could not have been sustained simply by imposing import controls. Whether a Conservative government would have devalued rather than cut back on internal growth is problematical, but highly unlikely. The incoming Labour Government chose not to do so.

Economic policies under the Labour Government

It was unfortunate that the first task of an inexperienced government taking office in October 1964 was to deal with a major crisis, and there is no doubt that an ineptitude in handling the situated added to the run on sterling. Probably, speculation against sterling was increased, for example, by an impression that the largely neutral budget of November 1964 was inflationary because it contained some welfare benefits; by the interpretation of panic given to the decision to raise Bank Rate on a Monday instead of the traditional Thursday; by the technical illegality of the imposition of an import surcharge; and by the mere fact that it was a Labour government which was in office. But the basic cause of the run was the large trade deficit which gave plausibility to the view that the pound was over-valued. The deficit could not be countered by the imposition of additional tariffs, or by the use of exchange controls, because Britain's obligations under various international arrangements—especially the G.A.T.T. and the I.M.F.—seemed to preclude such measures. Thus apart from devaluation the other main way of correcting the balance of payments deficit was by deflating the economy. Deflation, however, was a particularly difficult cause for Labour to espouse, both because of a long opposition to stop–go tactics and because the resultant increase in unemployment was distasteful. But the government gradually lurched in this direction over the next eighteen months.

The slowness of the acceptance of restraint undoubtedly added to the difficulties which ultimately had to be met. The budget of 1965 imposed higher indirect taxes (especially on drink and tobacco), which were reinforced by credit restraint and by direct measures to limit the export of capital. But the level of internal activity remained obstinately high and the trade balance worsened again in the middle of the year. This triggered off a further speculative run on sterling, which prompted more restraints—mainly on public investment and hire-purchase facilities. There was a brief gap in the external pressures—during which time a general election was held which returned the government with a more comfortable majority (97 instead of 3). But it became progressively clearer that the deflationary measures so far taken were not having the expected effects. The level of activity remained high, wage rates continued to rise rapidly—and so did imports. Some steps were taken to dampen these trends in Callaghan's post-election budget of May 1966.

The most important step was the introduction of the Selective Employment Tax (S.E.T.). This was a levy on employers related to the size of their labour force. It was also intended that the tax would weigh more heavily on services (hotels, laundries, shops, etc.) than on manufacturing industry, and hence would encourage a shift of labour away from the service trades and towards manufacturing industry. S.E.T. later became a major source of tax revenue, but it had no immediate effect on the difficulties facing the economy in the summer of 1966 because, although it was announced in May 1966, it was not brought into operation until September.

Events would not wait so long. The trade figures continued to be bad, and confidence in sterling was further weakened by the long seamen's strike from mid-May until early July. It was at this juncture that the government made its apparently final choice between devaluation and deflation. In July, in the midst of an intensive speculation against the pound, an exceptionally severe restrictive package was introduced. There was to be a freeze—imposed by statute—on incomes for six months followed by a similar period of severe restraint; the 'regulator' was used to raise purchase taxes;[13] strict controls were placed on prices; public expenditure was

13. The 'regulator', which was introduced by the Finance Act of 1961, bestowed on the government the authority to vary, by up to 10 per cent in either direction, the rates of purchase tax and the customs and excise duties on drink, tobacco, and petrol (i.e. an existing duty of 30 per cent could be varied between 27 and 33 per cent). The regulator made possible a more or less immediate change in the levels of a wide range of indirect taxes: it was thus a potentially powerful instrument for the short-term management of the economy.

to be cut; a limit on foreign travel expenditure of £50 was introduced; and hire-purchase restrictions tightened. Even so, the pressure on sterling was slow to lift—presumably a reflection of the view that the trouble was not temporary, but stemmed from a persistent British deficit.

Still, the impact of the deflationary measures, combined with the negotiation of new central bank defences for sterling and more favourable trade figures at the end of the year, produced some respite. Indeed, early in 1967 more attention was given to the possibility of unemployment getting out of hand—it had reached 2 per cent and was still rising—than to the renewed deficit on external account. On this assessment the budget of 1967 was mildly expansionist. There was less justification for the mid-summer relaxation of hire-purchase controls and the granting of higher pensions and family allowances, which were not offset by greater tax receipts.

By the time these measures were taken, the unemployment difficulties were overshadowed by the worsening trade situation, which had become clear and which was intensified by the closure of the Suez Canal in June arising out of the Israeli–Arab conflict. If, as the government still passionately protested, the maintenance of the external parity of sterling was unquestionable, then measures which could only lead to higher imports were inadmissible. Yet the various measures taken between June and August 1967 all tended to stimulate the level of internal demand.

The 1967 devaluation

The 14·3 per cent devaluation of sterling which finally came on 18th November owed little—except perhaps its timing—to these short-term adjustments. The long persistence of a trade deficit had gradually fashioned a widespread conviction that sterling was overvalued. As this view hardened, the deflationary alternative became less and less plausible for two main reasons. In the first place, the degree of deflation which would have been required would have been politically unacceptable. More important, however, it would not have provided a permanent solution to the situation. If, as it seemed, there was an underlying lack of British competitiveness in international markets at the existing exchange rate, then short-term deflationary measures would only have held this in check: any relaxation of the deflationary pressure would simply have led to a fresh external deficit.

Devaluation seemed the only practicable policy: it was not in itself a solution, however, but merely gave a respite. In this sense, the devaluation was in some respects well-arranged to secure a maximum benefit. It was accompanied by the provision of substantial international financial assistance to Britain to meet short-term difficulties, and most other countries had agreed to accept the move without adjusting their own economies, which would have reduced the comparative benefit to Britain.

Regional variations

The acute cleavage between the relatively depressed and the relatively prosperous regions of the British economy, which had been so marked a feature of the inter-war years, was enormously softened in the years after 1945. In historical terms it is the extent to which all regions enjoyed comparatively high levels of employment and prosperity which is probably the major point to notice about regional economic variations in Britain since the Second World War. But such perspectives tend only mildly to condition current attitudes and policies: in these terms, what needs to be noticed is that regional differences still persisted in the fifties and sixties, that they were *proportionately* still quite large, and that they excited considerable attention.

Some of the main economic differences between the regions of the United Kingdom may be suggested by Tables 5.3 and 5.4 which indicate the disparities in the rate of unemployment, and in the levels of earnings and household income. The unemployment figures have been widely used as indicators, and they show the continuance of the same basic pattern between rich and poor regions as had existed during the inter-war years. Indeed, the only substantial change in the inter-war order is that Wales was overtaken by Scotland as the region with the heaviest unemployment rate in Great Britain (i.e. excluding Northern Ireland). All of Southern England (except for the South West), the Midlands and the Yorkshire and Humber areas experienced rates of unemployment which were persistently below the national average. In the North-Western region unemployment was a little above the national average; in the North and in Wales the unemployment rate was normally rather less than double the national rate; in Scotland it was normally rather more than double; and in Northern Ireland it was between three and four times the national rate.

The information on earnings needs to be treated with more than

Table 5.3 Unemployment rates (percentage) new standard regions, 1958–70

Males and females	1958	1959	1960	1961	1962	1963	1964	1965	1966	1967	1968	1969	1970
United Kingdom	2·2	2·3	1·7	1·6	2·1	2·6	1·7	1·5	1·6	2·5	2·5	2·5	2·7
South East	⎱ 1·4	1·3	1·0	1·0	1·3	1·6	1·0	0·9 ⎱	1·0	1·7	1·6	1·6	1·7
East Anglia	⎰	1·3	1·0	1·4	1·7	2·1	1·5	1·3 ⎰	1·4	2·1	2·0	1·9	2·1
South West	2·2	2·1	1·7	1·4	1·7	2·1	1·5	1·6	1·8	2·5	2·5	2·7	2·8
West Midlands	⎱ 1·7	1·6	1·8	1·8	2·5	2·0	1·0	0·9 ⎱	1·3	2·5	2·2	2·0	2·3
East Midlands	⎰	1·3	1·1	1·1	1·8	2·0	1·0	0·9 ⎰	1·1	1·8	1·9	2·0	2·3
Yorks. & Humberside	⎰	1·8	1·6	1·6	2·2	3·1	2·1	1·1	1·2	2·1	2·6	2·6	2·9
North West	2·7	2·8	1·9	1·6	2·5	3·1	2·1	1·6	1·5	2·5	2·5	2·5	2·8
North	2·4	3·3	2·9	2·5	3·7	5·0	3·3	2·6	2·6	4·0	4·7	4·8	4·8
Wales	3·8	3·8	2·7	2·6	3·1	3·6	2·6	2·6	2·9	4·1	4·0	4·1	4·0
Scotland	3·8	4·4	3·6	3·1	3·8	4·8	3·6	3·0	2·9	3·9	3·8	3·7	4·3
Northern Ireland	9·3	7·8	6·7	7·5	7·5	7·9	6·6	6·1	6·1	7·7	7·2	7·3	7·0

Source: H.M.S.O., *Abstract of Regional Statistics*, No. 4, 1968 and No. 7, 1971.

Table 5.4 Earnings, hours of work, household income and number of persons per household, 1967

| | Given as percentage of U.K. average | | | |
	Weekly earnings[1]	Hours worked	Average weekly household income[2]	Number of persons per household
United Kingdom	100·0	100·0	100·0	3·02
South East	104·9	101·1	112·1	2·89
East Anglia	91·3	101·5	93·1	2·98
South West	96·4	100·7	92·1	2·98
West Midlands	104·0	96·2	109·0	3·08
East Midlands	97·0	100·0	98·8	3·10
Yorkshire & Humberside	92·9	101·3	95·8	2·96
North West	97·8	101·5	95·1	3·04
North	97·4	99·1	83·8	3·09
Scotland	97·0	100·7	94·8	3·22
Wales	101·8	97·4	90·3	3·03
N. Ireland	87·6	99·3		

Source: *Abstract of Regional Statistics*, No. 4, 1968.

1. Manufacturing Industries only   2. Average of 1964–7

Table 5.5   Regional distribution of expenditure, personal incomes, and gross domestic product at factor cost, 1961

	Given as proportion of U.K. average				G.D.P. per head £
	Personal income per head	Labour force at work as proportion of population of working age	Productivity of labour force at work	G.D.P. per head	
U.K.	100	100	100	100	454
North	82·6	92·0	98·9	91	411
E. & W. Ridings	94·0	100·7	98·1	100	453
N. Midlands	94·0	98·0	104·1	102	465
Midlands	103·4	104·0	101·8	108	489
South East	118·4	104·3	105·5	111	502
South West	94·8	93·1	96·0	88	400
North West	95·1	102·6	95·9	99	449
Wales	81·3	88·4	99·4	88	401
Scotland	84·2	96·0	90·7	86	389
N. Ireland	63·5	88·7	77·4	65	293

Source: *National Institute Economic Review*, No. 46, November 1968, p. 46.

usual caution for several reasons. For example, the information relates only to manufacturing industry, which is under-represented in some of the poorer regions. Moreover, the picture given by individual earnings may be quite different from that given by household incomes. Wales, for example, rated quite high in terms of earnings but was quite low in terms of household income, largely because the very poor employment opportunities for women meant that the average number of earners per household was low.

A more generalised, but an even more tentative, picture is given by Table 5.5 showing how personal incomes per head and gross domestic product per head in each of the regions compared with the average for the United Kingdom in 1961. The broad conclusion, however, is probably reliable enough, and chimes in with the other indicators. It is that Northern Ireland, Scotland, Wales, and the North were the regions which were most obviously relatively poor, while the Midlands and the South East were the relatively rich regions. This was no doubt a factor which contributed to the resurgence of nationalism in the 'Celtic fringe', particularly during the 1960s. Even so it is important to notice that the difference between 'rich' and 'poor' was not large—indeed, compared to other countries it was unusually small.[14] The differences would, moreover, probably be smaller than the tables indicate, if allowances were made for net transfer payments (via taxes, grants, and subsidies) and for regional price differences.

Despite their relative unreliability, data on earnings and incomes are particularly important because they are the basis of regional differences in the pressure of demand, which were a key factor in explaining the post-war inter-regional differences in employment and growth.[15] There were other factors, of course. The variations in industrial structure—some regions having a preponderance of declining industries and others of growing industries—were still important, but their significance had declined since the inter-war period. This was because regional specialisation markedly decreased, partly because some of the industries that were most highly concentrated in particular regions (coal-mining, shipbuilding, textiles,

14. A. J. Brown, 'Survey of . . . Regional Economics, with special reference to the United Kingdom', *Economic Journal*, LXXIX, 1969, p. 761.

15. Brown, Bowers, Cheshire, Lind, and Woodward, 'Regional Problems and Regional Policy', *National Institute Economic Review*, No. 46, November 1968, pp. 42 ff.

pottery) had greatly dwindled in relative importance.[16] Thus while the total working population increased from 19·4 million in 1921 to 27·0 million in 1966, the numbers engaged in coal-mining fell from 1·1 million to 0·4 million.

Regional problems and government policy

This was, indeed, another factor which made the regional differences less pronounced after 1945 than they had been during the inter-war years—in terms of the economic statistics, the concept of Britain as 'two nations' had much less validity. But, although the problem may thus seem to have diminished since 1945, the policies directed towards its cure have increased. The very wide regional differences of the inter-war years did provoke the Special Areas (Development and Improvement) Act of 1934, which was supplemented by further Acts in 1936 and 1937. These, however, did not create many new employment opportunities in the depressed regions. In the post-war period a wide range of policy instruments was devised to even out regional economic differences.

The broad policy, initiated by the Distribution of Industry Act of 1945 and the Town and Country Planning Act of 1947, was to single out particular districts or areas where unemployment was relatively high and to attempt to stimulate employment in them. The particular methods, like the areas concerned, were changed from time to time but they mostly fall into one of three broad categories:

(i) The use of restriction to prevent the expansion of existing firms, or the establishment of new firms in areas where the level of activity was already high. The intention was to squeeze such firms out of the prosperous regions and into the development areas. Apart from the use of building licences for this purpose in the immediate post-war years, the main instrument of restriction was the Industrial Development Certificate. An I.D.C. was required from the Board of Trade before the construction of any building for manufacturing industry above a minimum size (usually 5,000 square feet). Not much use was made of this restrictive control during the 1950s, but it was more widely employed in the following decade.

(ii) A more positive approach was through the direct provision of facilities by the government. For a few years after 1945 the government was able to offer factory space originally built for war purposes,

16. A. J. Brown, 'Survey of . . . Regional Economics', p. 777.

but this policy mostly took the form of the Board of Trade building factories in the development areas and offering them to firms at low rents.

(iii) The area of policy which fluctuated most was that of granting financial inducements to firms to move into development areas. Government encouragement of investment (at first through tax allowances, but towards the end of the 1960s through cash grants) discriminated strongly in favour of development areas. Loans and grants were also available to firms moving to such areas and, from September 1967, manufacturers in development areas received a regional employment premium of 30 shillings (£1·50) a week for each man employed full time.

It is not clear what effects these policies achieved. The regional differences were not noticeably any less in 1970 than they had been in the 1940s, but perhaps the policies prevented the divergencies from getting any wider. The policies were based on a philosophy of taking work to the workers, but the movement of people from the poorer to the most prosperous regions much exceeded the rate at which new jobs were created in the development areas. Once again, however, the situation would probably have been much worse without the policies. Indeed, all this suggests that there were powerful underlying forces making for increased regional differences and for movement from the less active to the more active regions. Government policy was perhaps necessary to check the increase in regional imbalance, an imbalance which was believed to be undesirable perhaps more on social and cultural than on economic grounds.

Chapter 6

The British Economy Since 1945: Some Explanations

The international setting

In the 1920s there had been strong and persistent attempts to rebuild the mechanism of the international economy. The attempts encountered formidable difficulties—the changed institutional basis of the gold standard, agricultural over-production, the distortions introduced by reparations and war debts—and eventually these efforts broke down between 1929 and 1933. Partly as a reaction to this, the international economy of the 1930s was severely constrained. Nearly all countries imposed more or less stringent restrictions on external trade and finance. A much greater importance was attached to maintaining stability in the internal economy and to restoring the level of domestic employment.

The hope after 1945 was to combine these two approaches by creating an expansive international economy which still left individual countries substantial freedom to control their own affairs. There was no likelihood at all that most individual countries would allow their internal economies to be dominated by external events. Keynesian economics had suggested that there was no need to do so —that it was possible and rational for governments to exercise some degree of control over the internal level of activity in their economies. By 1945, moreover, many countries were—or were soon to be— committed to exercising some such control, which was most usually expressed by making 'high' or 'full' employment a major policy objective. None the less there was also a strong desire to secure the gains and advantages which accrued from international trade. The intention was thus to create the mechanism and institutions which would secure these advantages to the fullest extent compatible with the right of individual countries to control their internal economies.

In general, there was a widespread acceptance that the advantages of international specialisation were best secured by a multilateral trading system and fully convertible currencies. The emphasis on multilateralism sprang from a recognition of the restraining effects of the bilateral trading arrangements which were so common in the 1930s. The tendency under bilateral trade is to require each country to balance its trade accounts individually with each of the countries with which it trades—in each case the balance has to be struck at the level of the country which wishes to import the smaller amount. Multilateral trade encourages a greater volume of international trade because it allows a country to use credits arising from trade with one country to pay for the deficits arising from trade with some other country. Thus multilateral trade needs free convertibility of currencies, since this is necessary to allow debts between any pair of countries to be settled through the transfer of a credit balance which the debtor country has accumulated in some third country.

The general aim, then, was to provide for an international economy based on multilateral trading and free convertibility of currencies. To this was often added, implicitly or explicitly, a desire for free trade. But it is important to notice that multilateral trade is not necessarily the same as free trade; free trade requires the absence of trade barriers, but multilateral trade is not incompatible with the existence of tariffs.

Some post-war international economic institutions

In the event, the post-war progress towards these aims of multilateral trade and currency convertibility was very slow despite some early agreement on institutions. As we have already seen (pp. 119–20), two of the basic post-war international economic institutions had been agreed as early as 1944. The World Bank was intended as a channel for international capital movements; the International Monetary Fund (I.M.F.) was meant to secure fixed exchange rates between the various national currencies.[1] In 1947 a further body— the General Agreement on Tariffs and Trade (G.A.T.T.)—was set up to work for the reduction of trade barriers. But none of these organisations contributed very much to the liberalisation of trade before the mid-fifties.

1. The intention was to avoid the currency chaos which arose from the competitive devaluations of, particularly, the early 1930s. I.M.F. members agreed to keep the exchange-rates of their currencies fixed. The I.M.F. mechanism, affording extra borrowing rights, was supposed to avoid the need for currencies to be adjusted because of short-term fluctuations. It was possible for countries faced with long-run difficulties to devalue their currencies, though this was supposed only to be done after consultation with the Fund.

The basic reason for this was the extent of the disruption which existed in 1945. The war had damaged and curtailed the network of world trade even more than had the Great Depression; and many important trading countries, particularly in Europe, emerged from it with their economies seriously weakened. Thus, although the principles of the I.M.F. and G.A.T.T. were widely accepted, the reality was that many countries—especially in the face of the overwhelming dominance of the United States in production and finance —could not conduct their external trade without a formidable array of tariffs, import quotas, and exchange controls. After the resounding failure of Britain's ill-starred 'dash for convertibility' in 1947, there was a general recognition that these restraints on international trade and finance would only be slowly dismantled.

The moves in this direction were often first made on a regional basis. In particular, steps taken between 1947 and 1957 towards a greater liberalisation of trade within Europe were an important prerequisite for a more general freedom of international trade. United States aid to Europe under the 1947 Marshall Plan formed the basis of this European initiative. The resultant Organisation for European Economic Co-operation (O.E.E.C.) served as a major centre through which successive steps towards liberalising intra-European trade were negotiated.

Britain was an active partner in these discussions to remove direct control over trade between European countries, but she did not take part when the process was pressed still further: the 1957 Treaty of Rome established the European Economic Community (Common Market) and was signed by representatives of the six countries: France, West Germany, Italy, Belgium, Luxembourg, and the Netherlands. The E.E.C., besides its far-reaching political objectives, was aimed at a full customs and economic union between its members.

A number of other European countries, who were at the time unable or unwilling to join the Common Market, formed in 1960 a second organisation, the European Free Trade Association (E.F.T.A.).[2] The aims of E.F.T.A. were more modest and less permanent than those of the E.E.C. The intention was to liberalise European trade and to reach an understanding with the Common Market. The latter is most likely to be achieved by some or all of the

2. Initially there were seven member countries: Austria, Denmark, Norway, Portugal, Sweden, Switzerland, and the United Kingdom. Finland and Iceland joined later.

E.F.T.A. countries joining the Common Market. Britain made a serious bid to do so in 1963 but, after prolonged negotiations, France vetoed Britain's application to enter the Community. In 1970 a new British effort to negotiate terms of entry was successfully launched, and Parliament voted for entry on October 24th, 1971.

Growth in currency convertibility

Side by side with the gradual relaxation of direct controls on intra-European trade in the 1950s, there was also a tendency to increase the degree of currency convertibility within Europe. The main organisation for this purpose was the European Payments Union (E.P.U.), established in 1950 by the O.E.E.C. The E.P.U. at once enabled the countries concerned to relax the restrictive bilateral balancing of trade. The E.P.U. granted limited credits to deficit members, while surplus members extended credit to the E.P.U. In effect there was thus a new pool of currency reserves which, since the inadequacy of the currency reserves of the various individual countries had been a major restraint on their external trade, encouraged an expansion of trade which tended both to multiply and to stimulate internal production. Gradually the restraints on currency convertibility within Europe declined and this paved the way towards a wider convertibility. At the end of 1958 most of the major European countries had restored full currency convertibility for non-residents.

An important factor contributing to the extension of currency convertibility was the decline of dollar scarcity. This was made possible by a number of factors. The vigorous revival of European production in the 1950s meant that the United States gradually ceased to be the sole or major source of supply for many products. In addition Europe was producing at prices which enabled it to compete directly with United States products. To some extent these factors derived part of their stimulus from the trend towards more freedom in European trade and finance. However, the ending of the dollar shortage also came from more autonomous factors: in particular, the growth of American military and aid expenditure overseas and the rise in private foreign investment by Americans were major sources of the greater availability of dollars.[3]

3. In the 1960s the international economy became more threatened by an excess of dollars than a shortage, that is, some countries became reluctant to hold dollars and this threatened to undermine confidence in the major international currency.

Stability of exchange rates

In many respects the really effective post-war restoration of the international economy dates from the general establishment of multilateral trade and free convertibility during the latter half of the 1950s. As a further result the international economic institutions—particularly the I.M.F., G.A.T.T., and the World Bank—then came into much greater prominence.

On the monetary side the influence of such institutions was exerted to support the Bretton Woods system whereby governments agreed to peg their currencies to gold or to the U.S. dollar (which was pegged to gold). The resultant stability of exchange rates was not, however, absolute—indeed, it is often referred to as the 'adjustable peg' system. A government could, under certain conditions, alter its exchange rate when its international accounts were in 'fundamental disequilibrium', a term that was left undefined. The aim was to secure relative stability of exchange rates while allowing needed changes to take place in an orderly manner and without provoking the kind of competitive devaluation which had taken place in the 1930s.

In the event, adjustments of the exchange rates of the major international currencies were rare. There were two main rounds—1949 and 1967—both of which were initiated by a devaluation of sterling (in 1949 from \$4·03 to \$2·80; in 1967 from \$2·80 to \$2·40). There were other alterations (such as the French devaluations of 1957 and 1969, and the revaluations of the German mark in 1961 and 1969), but governments were generally reluctant to change their exchange rates. They usually did so only after efforts to cut down on imports—either directly or by imposing deflation at home—had failed. There was also (see below pp. 180–4) a general shortage of international financial liquidity which similarly threatened to restrain the growth of world trade. In response to these difficulties a growing body of opinion in the 1960s advocated the case for more flexible exchange rates.[4] In 1970, however, all the major currencies—except for the Canadian dollar, which its government, repeating an experiment of the 1950s, allowed to fluctuate—were still committed to stable exchange rates. The continuing monetary crisis was, however, producing a major shift in attitudes and this was symbolised by the devaluation of the dollar in 1971.

4. See H. Katrak, *International Trade and the Balance of Payments* (Chapter 4) in this series.

Moves towards freer trade

On the trade side, G.A.T.T. continued in the 1960s its attempts to reduce the barriers to world trade. In particular, the so-called 'Kennedy Round' of negotiations—initiated in 1962 and completed in 1967—led to average tariff levels in Britain, the E.E.C., and the U.S. being reduced by about one-third. Substantial problems still remained. For example, very little progress was made in reducing the level of agricultural protection in industrialised countries, and this especially disappointed the less developed countries seeking markets for their primary products. But progress was considerable. Tariffs were reduced, and quantitative restrictions on trade were largely confined to the less developed countries or to a few particular products, like textiles. These steps helped to make the post-war period one in which world trade flourished.

An assessment of performance

In many ways the post-war performance of the British economy was highly satisfactory. As we have already seen, the rate of growth of real national product was higher than in both the inter-war period and the years before 1913 (p. 56, note 17). The better performance was achieved, moreover, with a much more continuously upward trend than had ever been experienced before 1939. Before the Second World War, the fairly regular occurrence of years in which there was a fall in national output, in absolute terms and not just in its rate of growth, was considered to be unavoidable—and even indispensable for inducing the structural changes required of a growing economy. After 1945, however, the economy grew—not steadily, certainly— but virtually without any of these periods of falling national output with their accompaniment of economic disruption and distress for many people. Even industrial production, a much more volatile indicator, showed only a few occasional, and very marginal, declines (in 1952 and 1958).

Full employment

Closely associated with the upward trend in the national product, and in even more marked contrast to the inter-war period, was the maintenance of a very high level of employment. Indeed, the average annual level of unemployment was, for more than a generation, kept below what Beveridge in 1944 considered to be a minimum possible level of 3 per cent. In addition, as already noted, the absolute levels of the regional variations, though still pronounced, were much more muted, so that the enjoyment of the growth of economic output was geographically much more widely distributed than it was before 1939. The whole process was, moreover, accompanied by adjustments which made the industrial structure better adapted to contemporary needs. For example, one of the less noticed but quite substantial post-war economic achievements was the extraordinarily peaceful way in which a substantial run-down in the size of the coal-mining industry was effected.

Such substantial elements of satisfaction in the British economic record were given more prominence in the 1950s than has since been the case. There are two main reasons for this. Firstly, there was between the 1950s and the 1960s a significant change of emphasis in the priorities given to different economic objectives; and, secondly, the economy was more successful in satisfying the expectations of the 1950s than it was in meeting those of the following decade. At the cost of much oversimplification, the essential point may be made by saying that for a decade or so immediately after the war there was a major concern with the maintenance of full employment, which gradually became replaced by an uneasiness over what came to be seen as an inadequate rate of growth. (The persistent pre-occupation with balance of payments issues was concerned with means rather than ends, though there were times enough when this seemed to be forgotten.)

It is not difficult to understand the initial anxiety over full employment. The traumatic economic experience of Britain in the inter-war years was the emergence and almost continuous persistence of unemployment on a scale much greater than had previously existed. A number of other countries—virtually all advanced industrial countries—experienced widespread unemployment between the wars. But in few did this experience leave its mark as deeply as in Britain. This was because most other countries either had substantial periods —especially in the 1920s—of reasonably high employment; or they had experiences of an even more disrupting nature—such as the hyper-inflation experienced in Germany in 1923 which, especially as its memory was reinforced by a similar experience in 1947–48, tended to make the avoidance of inflation seem even more important in the post-war years then the avoidance of unemployment.

For these reasons, the commitment to maintain full employment, which became a general undertaking in many countries after 1945, was taken with especial seriousness in Britain. Even so, few thought at the time of the Beveridge White Paper of 1944 that the commitment to full employment—even when defined as involving a minimum of 3 per cent unemployed—could be much more than a pious hope. It was seen as a target to aim for, but with no great expectation that it would be reached—let alone surpassed. In the event, the maintenance of full employment has been perhaps the most robust of the post-war economic trends. But it is important to recall the more fragile contemporary view because it helps to explain both the persistent stress placed upon this objective, and the satisfaction which for a time accompanied its attainment.

Rising consumers' expenditure

Some of the other basic wishes of the post-war period—relief from the austerities of war, and a rise in the long suppressed level of real consumers' expenditure—were reasonably realised, especially in the 1950s. Some such improvements were inevitable as men and resources were released from war purposes and diverted to peacetime production and activity. The war had, however, bitten deeper than was generally realised, and the pace of increase in consumers' expenditure initially fell behind expectations.

In the 1950s the pace was substantially quickened. In part this reflected the fuller readjustment to peace; in part it represented the upward trend in national output. But it also went beyond these, since the level of income available to consumers after tax rose faster than total national output. Such an outcome was largely fortuitous: it arose from a very considerable decline in the proportion of output which went to defence (from nearly 10 per cent in 1953 to 7 per cent in 1957), and from the favourable terms of trade which enabled Britain to secure more imports for the same volume of exports.

Increasing disappointment over economic performance

Any satisfaction felt with these improvements, however, dimmed with the passage of time. Full employment came to be taken so much for granted that any lapses from the high standards which had been set were politically explosive. Attention began to be turned towards other economic problems. Thus, although fluctuations in unemployment were constrained within narrow limits, the jerky nature of the progress of the economy as a whole could not be disguised. Certainly, one thing that emerges with abundant clarity, even from the brief narrative of the previous chapter, is that the management of the economy tended to produce frequent changes of direction. The disquiet at the nature of the stop–go progression was, moreover, associated with a mounting realisation that the British economy was growing less rapidly than most others. In the international growth 'league tables', which became especially fashionable at the end of the 1950s, Britain consistently emerged at the bottom end. It became increasingly appreciated, moreover, that—even though it was rising at an historically favourable rate—the British standard of living was declining relative to that of other advanced industrial countries.

Any assessment of the performance of the economy would thus have to include consideration of these trends. Indeed, much of the widely held impression that the post-war performance was inadequate derives largely from a feeling that the economy has lurched from crisis to crisis, combined with a resentment that its rate of growth fell behind that of other Western European countries. Why there should have been such shortcomings is not easy to answer. There have been, partly because of the general dissatisfaction, many close examinations of the British economy, but it would be misleading to suggest that any universally accepted explanation has emerged from these multitudinous probings. There is only agreement that a number of factors have been at work. Some of the more important of these are mentioned below.

Some major influences on British economic performance

1. *The effect of the war*

The conversion of the economy to the needs of war was even more complete between 1939 and 1945 than it had been in the First World War. There were fewer casualties but more damage, since not just Britain's ships, but her towns and cities, ports and factories, were more accessible to enemy attack. In general, however, there were three major ways in which the disruptions of war exerted an influence upon the economy.

In the first place, there was the loss of capital equipment. Such capital losses resulted less from direct destruction than from the neglect of the maintenance and replacement of such equipment as was not considered essential for the conduct of the war. The war years thus saw a vast consumption of capital equipment, instead of the more normal net annual accumulation of capital.

In the second place—and connected with the point just made—the war produced significant distortions in the industrial structure. Industries which made a direct contribution to war—such as armaments, aircraft, and shipbuilding—were expanded, while the relative importance of others dwindled drastically.

Such tendencies, however, were clearly not confined to Britain, nor was their impact obviously on a greater scale or more disruptive than in several other countries. In addition, there were several off-setting factors, such as the substantial technical discoveries and applications which had been quickened by the demands of war. Moreover, in Britain as elsewhere, the capital back-log was—especially with the aid provided under the Marshall Plan—made good fairly rapidly, while some sectors of industry—electrical engineering, plastics, and man-made fibres—had been given a helpful wartime boost which probably improved the appropriateness of the industrial structure. Certainly, the depressing effects arising from these wartime influences must have substantially spent themselves by 1950.

The third major disruption stemming from the war has had more permanent and far-reaching effects. It relates to the impact of the war on Britain's overseas assets. The war was responsible for two trends, each of which was highly unfavourable. It led to a substantial sale of foreign investments—particularly before the introduction of lease–lend—in order to pay for essential imports of food, raw materials, and arms. By 1945 about half (£1,200 million) of Britain's pre-war foreign investments had been sold.

In addition, however, and to a far greater extent, Britain had run up substantial debts with a number of countries—especially India and countries in the Middle East—for supplies and services rendered, often to British troops stationed in these regions. These amounted to nearly £3,500 million. The joint effect of these two trends was to produce the dramatic effect of making Britain, for a time, a net debtor on overseas capital account, reversing a situation whereby for a century and a half overseas investment earnings had made a significant contribution to Britain's trading balance. Further reference to this factor will be made below (see p. 174) but for the moment it is sufficient to indicate that this constituted for Britain the most serious and stubborn of the legacies of war.

2. *An over-commitment to full employment?*

As the centre of concern shifted from the maintenance of full employment to anxiety over the rate of growth, the view began to be put forward that the economy was being run at too high a level of employment. Essentially, the argument here is that a low level of unemployment makes for a rapid rise in wage rates. This in turn pushes up the level of costs. Prices also rise because they are, by and large, related to costs. Not only does the higher level of prices then tend to lead to further wage demands, starting something of a wage-price spiral, but the higher prices also reduce the competitiveness of British exports and so increase the balance of payments difficulties. Several studies[5] have shown that there is something in this argument, and it lies at the basis of a frequently recurring suggestion—most closely associated with Professor Paish[6]—that the economy should be run at a lower level of capacity, implying a higher level of unemployment, in the belief that this would slow down the rate of wage and price increases and improve the balance of payments.

There are, however, a number of offsetting considerations. For example, any gains would have to be set against the decrease in total national output that would probably arise from the increase in unemployment. Moreover, the post-war experience of inflation was a general phenomenon: but some countries, notably West Germany in the 1960s, managed to combine a *lower* level of unemployment than Britain with a *lower* rate of price inflation and a *higher* rate of growth. More generally, although wage-costs rose more rapidly in Britain than in most other industrial countries, this was not mainly because wage-rates rose faster. It was because productivity rose more slowly in Britain. Finally, the experience of the early 1970s, when there was both a rising rate of inflation and a rising rate of unemployment, necessarily raised questions about the whole argument.

3. *The relatively slow growth of productivity*

There is much evidence that the failure of Britain's economic development to keep pace with that of other European countries and of the United States sprang largely from lagging productivity growth.[7]

5. See, for example, L. A. Dicks-Mireaux, 'The inter-relationships between cost and price changes', *Oxford Economic Papers*, October 1961.

6. See, for example, F. W. Paish and J. Henessey, *Policy for Incomes*, Hobart Paper No. 29, 1967.

7. A highly technical attempt to quantify this and other influences is to be found in Edward Dennison, *Why Growth Rates Differ*, 1967.

Productivity is, in any exact sense, a subtle and elusive concept. Here, however, all that is indicated is the ratio of total output (the gross domestic product) to total employment.

Used in this way (as a measure of output per employee), it is hardly surprising to find an association between economic growth and productivity. Indeed, lagging productivity could be said to be more a symptom than a cause: if the size of the population and the size of the working force change at the same rate, then increases in output per head amount to much the same thing as increases in productivity (meaning more output for each unit of input). It is not, however, easy to see with any certainty why productivity growth in Britain was lower than in other countries.

One possible explanation is that the quality of British management was relatively low. This turns largely on a belief that a career in management was accorded less prestige and status in Britain than in the United States or on the Continent, and hence failed to attract the highest talent. Judgments on this tend usually to be impressionistic in tone, but there is also some firmer evidence. In particular, it has been shown that American-owned subsidiary firms, working in Britain, earned something like a 50 per cent higher rate of return on assets than did their British-controlled competitors working in the same general environment.[8] Management performance remains a difficult factor to assess and quantify, but it seems at least likely that British management has been relatively inferior in its economic motivation and achievement.

There were other possible defects of organisation. Thus if the degree of monopoly had been unusually high in Britain, or if the average size of plant had been extremely low (limiting the benefits from economies of scale), these influences would have tended to depress the level of productivity. There is not much foundation in fact for either of these possibilities since, at least in relation to other industrialised European countries, British industry was not exceptionally monopolised, nor was the average factory unusually small.

Another possibility is that the trade unions have acted in ways that have tended to slow down growth. On this matter, a great deal of evidence exists to suggest that both the strength and the attitudes of the trade unions made for a persistence of productivity-reducing restrictive practices. The system of industrial relations was in general

8. J. H. Dunning, 'U.S. Subsidiaries in Britain and their U.K. Competitors', quoted in R. E. Caves, *Britain's Economic Prospects*, 1968, p. 300.

unsatisfactory, and contributed to the difficulty of raising productivity levels.

Industrial relations difficulties sprang from a complex of causes. One of the most prominent was the inappropriateness of the trade union structure. There were too many unions, most of which were too small. There were too many craft unions (unions bringing together all the members of a particular craft regardless of the industry within which they were employed) and too few unions organised along industrial lines (bringing together all the workers, whatever their craft, in a particular industry). The shop stewards had too much autonomy—although, contrary to popular mythology, they generally exercised this in a responsible and conscientious way.

Moreover, the whole bargaining process—which was usually initially between national federations of employers and national trade union leaders—placed too much emphasis on national wage bargains, which then served as a floor from which plant bargaining began. The tendency of this process to raise costs was greatly increased by the general reluctance of management—in an inflationary environment—to resist pressures for wage increases. Finally, the whole atmosphere of industrial relations was not conducive to the efficient use of labour, but it would be difficult to quantify this.

The influence of the public sector on productivity. It is sometimes argued that the large size of the public sector in Britain accounts for the comparative inefficiency of the economy. The most common basis for this assertion has rested on comparisons which take as their criterion of efficiency the rate of return on the capital invested, and this has generally been lower in the public sector than in private industry. Besides, in the post-war period the public sector has normally accounted for something approaching one-half of total investment in Britain,[9] thus—it is claimed—pushing down the average rate of return on capital.

The depressive effect of public sector investment is said to stem from two main sources. Firstly, a substantial proportion of this investment went into developments which were not directly produc-

9. U.K. public investment as a percentage of total investment, 1950–1966:

1950	30·6	1955	41·5	1960	56·2	1965	43·0	1970	45·1
1951	49·9	1956	58·3	1961	37·0	1966	46·5		
1952	55·8	1957	38·9	1962	40·2	1967	49·8		
1953	51·0	1958	38·3	1963	40·2	1968	48·1		
1954	40·7	1959	39·4	1964	42·9	1969	45·5		

tive—like housing and education and the health services. And secondly, because public investment in the more immediately productive spheres—in such nationalised industries as coal-mining, gas, electricity, and railways—frequently did not have to justify itself on any stringent test about the rate of return on the capital involved. Until the second half of the 1950s, for example, the general coal shortage meant that much investment in coal-mining was made largely on the simple grounds that it would increase output.

All these points have provoked counter-arguments. Thus it is pointed out that the size of the public sector was proportionately just as large in a number of other countries which none the less sustained a faster rate of economic growth than Britain. The same point could be made about the level of investment in 'non-productive' social services—in the 1950s, for example, a greater proportion of total investment went into housing in West Germany than in Britain. In addition, a number of recent studies have at least cast doubt on the proposition that the rate of return on capital invested in 'non-productive' services, like education, is lower than it is in industry. And, in the 1960s at least, investment projects in the nationalised industries were subjected to much more scrutiny. Two important White Papers established the principle that such proposals should, judged by modern techniques of investment appraisal, yield an anticipated return of 8 per cent, and that the pricing policies of these industries should be based on economic, rather than social, criteria.[10]

It is at least doubtful, then, whether much of the low level of productivity in post-war Britain can be attributed to the amount of capital invested in the public sector. A related, but more generalised, approach has emphasised that the overall level of British investment, public and private, was inadequate.

4. A deficiency in the amount of capital invested

Although the measurement of investment involves many difficulties, a whole series of studies has pretty firmly established that the proportion of the national income which was devoted to investment in

10. *Financial Objectives of Nationalised Industries* (Cmnd. 1337), 1961 and *Nationalised Industries: a review of Economic and Financial Objectives.* (Cmnd. 3437), 1967. A recent study also suggests that, for the 1960s especially, the rate of growth of labour productivity in nationalised industries compared favourably with that in private manufacturing industry. R. W. S. Pryke, 'Are Nationalised Industries becoming more efficient?', *Moorgate and Wall Street*, Spring 1970.

Britain was below that of most other major industrial countries.[11] As a result there was a retarded rate of growth of the capital stock. But, in addition, it is said that the absolute level of capital stock was low—indeed, that fixed enterprise capital per worker was lower in Britain than in almost any other country in Western Europe.[12]

There is a close relationship between the level of investment and the level of output.[13] Indeed, the much higher output per worker in the United States, compared with Europe, is frequently attributed almost entirely to the greater amount of capital per worker in the United States. But the relationship between investment and output, though highly important, is not as direct and clear-cut as it is sometimes presented. If, for example, the average age of the capital equipment is high then a substantial proportion of it will need replacement each year. As a result, out of a given level of gross investment, more is used for simple maintenance and less is available for making net additions to the capital stock than would be the case if the average age of the capital stock was low.

There is a widely-held presumption that Britain has suffered from these depressive effects of an older capital stock. But, in any event, the broad empirical evidence for Britain raises substantial doubts about the directness of any connection between investment and output. The proportion of gross investment to gross national product rose from about 15 per cent in the 1950s to about 20 per cent in the 1960s. But this does not seem to have been accompanied by an increase in the rate of growth of output in Britain. Moreover, although the higher proportion of gross national product which was invested represented a closing of the gap between the investment ratio in Britain and that in other European countries, Britain's rate of economic growth did not catch up but, if anything, lagged still further behind.

The empirical evidence thus serves as a warning against drawing too firm and direct a line between investment ratios and an increase in total output. This said, it still remains true that the lower level of investment in Britain helps to explain its apparently unsatisfactory

11.

	Japan	W. Ger.	France	U.S.	U.K.
Gross investment as % of G.N.P. (ave. 1955–64)	28·8	23·7	19·2	17·1	15·8

12. R. E. Caves, *Britain's Economic Prospects*, 1968, p. 272.

13. For the theoretical basis for this see Chapter 5 of Ford, *Income, Spending and the Price Level*, in this series.

post-war economic performance. The question still remains as to why the level of investment was low. It does not seem to be explicable in terms of the tax structure. For most of the post-war period taxes on corporate profits were low in Britain compared to the United States; and, in addition, British fiscal policy—through investment allowances and premiums, especially in the less prosperous regions— gave strong positive inducements to invest.

A more important cause was probably the stop–go effects of government policy. The level of investment in the private sector depends in part on the expectations which businessmen hold about the future. If they expect the demand for their products to expand quickly and continuously they will be encouraged in their plans to expand capacity. But in post-war Britain the frequent attempts by government policy to cut back or curb the level of demand introduced much uncertainty as to its future level which discouraged investment, especially long-term investment. The criticism arising from the alleged disruptions of a stop–go policy is, moreover, sometimes broadened into the suggestion that the shortcomings of government economic policy generally were a substantial cause of a poor rate of economic development.

5. *The management of the economy as a source of its difficulties*

In some senses, as already mentioned, the post-war management of the economy was outstandingly successful. The variations in fiscal and, to a lesser extent, monetary policy constrained the fluctuations in activity within very narrow limits and close to a full employment level. None the less, as the previous chapter has indicated, the changes in policy direction were frequent, and perhaps sometimes created an impression of being sharper and fiercer than they actually were. Moreover, government policies were often faulty in their timing—as, for example, in the budgetary boost which was given to the already strong investment boom of 1955. To the extent that government policies gave the wrong signals at the wrong times, or gave too strong (or too weak) a signal, or gave too many signals, it could be said that these policies themselves introduced a degree of instability and uncertainty which tended to hold back development in the long run.

Of course, the management of the economy is a very inexact art. It may be that its practice is improving as something is learned from past experience, new theoretical insights become available, fuller information is provided and made available sooner,[14] and new instruments of control are devised. In the quarter century since 1945, however, there was not much change in the basic system of economic management: fundamentally this involved the management of the total level of demand by using fiscal and, to a lesser extent, monetary policies.[15]

Partly this is because of the shortcomings of the possible alternatives. In Britain there was some experimentation with two of these: economic planning and incomes policy. Economic planning is a term much more frequently used than defined—perhaps because it is too elusive a concept to be neatly and briefly pinned down. It might, however, be hazarded that the essential elements seem to be three: an attempt to indicate broad objectives which are within the capacity of the economy and which are to be aimed at within a given time span; an indication that the projections which this involves for the different sectors of the economy are co-ordinated and consistent; and the fashioning of specific policy measures to ensure that the projections are realised.

The first time that anything remotely satisfying these criteria was initiated in Britain was in the early 1960s and by a Conservative government. This was doubly significant. The timing was important since it came just when the realisation became widespread that Britain's post-war economic growth—though continuous—was lagging relative to that of other countries. And the Conservative initiative indicated that economic planning was no longer associated only with the political left.[16] Thus in 1961 Selwyn Lloyd established the National Economic Development Council (N.E.D.C.) as a body, independent of the Treasury, in which the government, the employers

14. Mr. Macmillan when he was Chancellor complained about the difficulties of working with 'last year's Bradshaw'.

15. Over the period as a whole the importance attached to the use of monetary policy has varied quite widely. After its virtual complete neglect in the 1940s it was given much greater prominence in the following decade while, over time, new tools of monetary policy—such as the use of special deposits—were evolved. None the less, monetary policy was primarily used to supplement fiscal policy, rather than as the dominant instrument of control.

16. The model for the British experiment was the French system of indicative planning. This in theory simply 'indicates' to the private sector—by constructing projections of future levels of demand and resources—the rate and nature of the expansion that is feasible and desirable. In practice, this permissiveness in the private sector is somewhat illusory: the French authorities have substantial indirect means at their disposal for inducing the private sector to act along the lines laid down in the plans.

and the trade unions (the T.U.C. agreed to take part in January 1962) could come together to examine the targets for economic growth, and ways in which obstacles to growth could be removed.

Some of the functions of the N.E.D.C. were, after the election of a Labour government in 1964, transferred to the Department of Economic Affairs (D.E.A.). This was set up under a senior Cabinet Minister, George Brown, to give high status to a body—set apart from the Treasury—which would be responsible for medium-term planning. But as time went on its significance rapidly waned. This was partly because the philosophy to which it was wedded—the philosophy of making rapid economic growth a largely overriding criterion—was inappropriate to the time, or, at least, was not adopted by the government as a whole. Instead the government made its major objective the avoidance of balance of payments difficulties at the existing exchange rate.

Rapid growth and the maintenance of the existing exchange rate for sterling were probably incompatible objectives for much of the 1960s, and especially for the second half of the decade. This was because, with the balance of payments situation already precarious, any increase in the rate of internal growth would, initially at least, have involved a substantial increase in the level of imports: but any aggravation of the external deficit had to be avoided if the exchange rate was to be maintained.

Such considerations contributed to the lack of success of the concept of economic planning in Britain during the 1960s. Two plans were published—the N.E.D.C. Plan for the five years up to 1966, and the National Plan published in 1965 to cover the years up to 1970. Neither greatly influenced policy, partly because their policy proposals were only loosely related to the projection exercises, and partly because they failed to carry credibility: they assumed more adeptness at containing price increases and averting balance of payments difficulties than was in fact achieved.

This links up with the second line along which attempts were made to supplement the mechanism for economic management in Britain—the use of incomes policy. This was seen as a means of eliminating or restricting inflationary trends and thus—if the rate of British price increases could be kept below that of other countries—of improving the balance of payments by making exports more competitive. This type of approach was fashionable in the 1960s but—like planning, of which it in some respects forms a part—incomes policy was greatly discussed but little practised. There were a few dramatic short-term interventions in this field. On several occasions (1948, 1956, 1961, and 1966) a 'wage-freeze' was imposed, more or less prohibiting all wage increases for some specified period. But these were mainly crisis reactions.

A more continuous approach began with the establishment in 1957 of a Council on Prices, Productivity, and Incomes, but this body mainly contented itself with broad reports on these issues. The first explicit steps towards a more permanent incomes policy dated from a White Paper of 1962. This was intended to provide a 'guiding light' for wage increases based upon the observed rate of productivity increase in preceding years—about 2 to $2\frac{1}{2}$ per cent.

The following year the National Incomes Commission, which had been established to scrutinise wage claims, raised the norm to 3 to $3\frac{1}{2}$ per cent on the basis that this higher rate of increase had been projected in the Plan issued by the N.E.D.C. This was largely repeated in the Labour Government's White Paper (*Prices and Incomes Policy*) issued in 1965. On this occasion more emphasis was placed on restraining prices in order to counter the—largely well-founded—criticism that incomes policy was mainly a euphemism for wages policy—prices, dividends, rents, and even salaries being given much less attention. A National Board for Prices and Incomes (the P.I.B.) was set up in 1965 to interpret the policy.

The policy did not have much success. During the 1960s wage rates rose by nearly 50 per cent (earnings by about 70 per cent) and prices by 40 per cent. The pace of increase, indeed, tended to quicken in the second half of the sixties despite the government's greater attempts to follow a more coherent incomes policy. There were many reasons for this. Thus it is probable that the longer inflationary trends continued, the more wage claims were likely to become larger, and to be made at shorter intervals, simply to discount the expectation of further price increases. It is also very difficult in judging changes in incomes to evolve criteria which combine economic sense, social justice, and general acceptability.

The policy, moreover, largely relied on 'ear-stroking' techniques: but exhortation and persuasion, rarely very effective, tend to erode rapidly over time. In particular trade unions tended not to exercise much restraint in making demands. There was formal co-operation. The T.U.C. in March 1965 agreed to the 3 to $3\frac{1}{2}$ per cent norm for wage increases; and six months later it set up an 'early warning system' for wage claims. In 1967 it undertook to vet such claims; and in 1969—as a counter to a mild government proposal to impose some more direct curbs on individual unions—accepted an obligation to intervene in unofficial strikes and disputes between unions.

But all this was not very effective. There is some evidence that short-term wage freezes did slow down wage increases, but there is no clear indication that this could be given greater durability by a longer-term voluntary incomes policy. The attempts to move towards some use of an incomes policy had, in effect, all arisen out of efforts to resolve balance of payments difficulties—to prevent high levels of employment leading to price increases which endangered external competitiveness. An examination of incomes policy, like all other roads of enquiry into the post-war British economy, leads in the end back to the balance of payments problem.

6. *Balance of payments difficulties*

There is no escaping the fact that the form in which Britain's economic shortcomings most characteristically revealed themselves was in external payments crises. Repeatedly the restrictive policies of the government were a response to a precarious balance of payments situation. A frequent pattern was for there to be a weakening of the current balance of payments,[17] which led to a much magnified withdrawal of foreign funds from Britain as a speculation against the existing dollar value of sterling. British governments tended to respond by imposing restrictions on the level of activity at home to keep down the level of imports, and to use a high rate of interest to attract foreign funds.

It is clear from the repetition of this basic pattern that the level of the British reserves of gold and foreign exchange was inadequate to meet the strains imposed. Why was this so? It could be because the basic balance of trade or current balance of payments had not been favourable, or not been favourable enough. Or it could be that the country was trying to perform functions—such as providing aid or investment overseas, maintaining an overseas military force, or allowing the pound to serve as an international currency—for which

17. In rough terms, the *balance of trade* shows the payments made and received because of current imports and exports of actual goods (visible trade); the *balance of payments on current account* includes this but also adds the trade in services, like banking, insurance, and shipping (invisible trade); the *balance of payments on capital account* records all other transactions—mainly capital transfers (government and private) and changes in the stocks of gold and foreign exchange. See also Katrak, Chapter 2. As indicated below (pp. 177–80), crises have also originated in or been aggravated by problems on capital account.

its reserves were insufficient. Or it could be that the absence of any solution to the general problem of international liquidity (see pp. 180–4) placed an extra strain on sterling and thus on Britain's external balance. The difficulties, of course, probably stem from some combination of all these factors, but it is perhaps more sensible to try and look at them separately.

(a) *The balance of trade*. The post-war balance of trade was, in many respects, remarkably good. For over a century before the Second World War Britain's balance of trade had been consistently unfavourable. Indeed, just before the war, in the years 1935 to 1938, Britain's visible exports paid on average for only two-thirds of her imports. In the 1950s visible exports paid for just over 94 per cent, and in the 1960s just under 94 per cent, of imports. This much faster growth of the value of exports compared to the value of imports in the post-war years was helped by the continuance of some restrictions on imports up to the second half of the 1950s, but it still represented a very substantial achievement.

None the less, in relation to the presumed need to keep a substantial surplus on the current balance—to invest abroad, pay off overseas debts, and enable sterling to serve as an international currency —the achievement was inadequate. Viewed from this standpoint, exports were too low or imports too high, or both. This aspect became increasingly relevant in the 1960s when, reversing the post-war trend, the value of imports grew as fast as, or faster than, that of exports.

An explanation commonly offered for such failings in Britain's visible trade balance has stressed the structure of Britain's foreign trade. Thus, for example, it is said that a high proportion of Britain's exports were directed towards countries whose economies were not growing very rapidly. Alternatively (or additionally), it is asserted that among British exports there was a high proportion of goods for which the growth in world demand was relatively slow.

There is some evidence to support these structural arguments. Thus nearly 29 per cent of British exports in 1968 went to the overseas sterling area (mainly the relatively slow-growing Commonwealth countries). The more significant point, however, was that a decade earlier this region had accounted for 42 per cent of British exports. In the same period the proportion of Britain's exports going to the fast-growing Western European markets had increased from 27 to 37 per cent. British exports were clearly being quite successfully redirected towards the faster growing markets. Similarly, increasingly significant among the products which Britain exported were such commodities as chemicals and vehicles for which demand was growing strongly. It seems likely, then, that only a part of Britain's export short-comings could be satisfactorily explained in these structural terms.

It seems much more plausible to argue that the trends in the balance of trade reflected the trends in British costs relative to those of other countries.[18] During the 1960s British unit costs rose faster than those of her main trading rivals, and this tended to stimulate imports and discourage exports. The importance of these price trends received some confirmation from the strongly favourable effects of the devaluation of November 1967 upon the balance of trade in 1968. The influence of price effects is a strong argument for an effective incomes policy—or for some other means of keeping the increases in British unit costs within the bounds imposed by her major competitors.

(b) *The balance of payments on current account.* Whereas the balance of trade is concerned with the import and export of goods, the current balance also includes trade in so-called invisibles—in services (such as banking, insurance, shipping, and tourism); in the return (interest or profit) on capital lent to or borrowed from abroad; in government services and in transfers. These invisible items have historically been extremely important in Britain's current balance of payments. Before 1913, Britain's overseas earnings from invisibles were large enough to convert a normally adverse balance of trade into a strongly favourable balance of payments on current account, the surplus then being used to increase British capital investment overseas.

In this respect the impact of the two world wars was of crucial importance. They, and especially the second, involved the sale of many overseas capital assets, the earnings from which had made so important a contribution to the trade balance. Britain sold something over £1,100 million in foreign assets during the Second World War, and income from foreign investments fell from just over £200 million before the war to £80 million in 1946. In addition the U.K. gold reserves fell during the war by about £150 million, and a massive foreign debt of £3,355 million was incurred. The resultant vast

18. In addition, British exports were often uncompetitive in terms of design, finish, servicing, and delivery dates. S. J. Wells, *British Export Performance*, 1964, p. 198.

decline in net external assets deprived Britain of a useful cushion to ease the inevitable post-war adjustments in her trading position.

Although income from overseas investment again mounted with the renewal of an outward flow of capital in the post-war years, and although the earnings from other services also increased, such improvements tended to be partially offset by a continuance of government expenditure abroad on a scale very much higher than had been known before 1939. As a result, the proportional contribution from the invisible items to the current balance deteriorated sharply. In 1913 the earnings from invisibles amounted to 40 per cent of the total value of British imports, and between 1935 and 1938 were still on average sufficient to pay for nearly one-third of the import bill. But during the 1960s Britain's net income from invisible trade could only have financed something less than one-twentieth of her imports.

(c) *The export of capital.* It is sometimes suggested that a contributory factor to Britain's external payments difficulties was the export of capital. From the early 1950s to the end of the 1960s the net outflow (i.e. allowing for investment in Britain by foreigners) averaged about £160 million a year, despite the fact that investment overseas remained subject to some degree of control throughout the post-war period. The argument is that such extensive outflows imposed a further strain on an already difficult balance of payments situation.

The counter to this argument rests on the assertion that foreign investment helps the balance of payments by contributing to earnings from interest and profits reaped abroad, and also that investment overseas often results in export orders for Britain. A recent study,[19] however, has indicated that the rate of return on foreign investment seems to compare unfavourably with investment at home. This increases the force of the basic point that, while foreign investment may be desirable, it may still be imprudent to aggravate acute short-term payments difficulties in order to finance investment whose gains will accrue mainly in the long run.

(d) *Sterling as an international currency.* The issues involved here are much more fundamental. Sterling has been used as an international currency for a long time. Before 1914, much of world trade, even when it was trade which did not directly involve a British buyer or seller, was conducted in terms of sterling, and the accounts were

19. W. B. Reddaway, *The Effects of United Kingdom Direct Investment Overseas*, 1967.

settled in London. The situation was modified between the wars when Britain's relative trading position declined. It was, however, still sufficient to make sterling important in world trade, and it was still reinforced by London's continued—though diminished—importance as a financial centre. The partial decline in the traditional reasons for holding sterling was, in any case, offset by the emergence of new reasons. Thus the gold exchange standard introduced after 1925 encouraged some countries to hold their reserves, not in gold, but in currencies which were directly linked to gold (which usually meant either sterling or the dollar). And even when the United Kingdom left the gold standard in 1931 a number of countries—mainly in the Commonwealth and Scandinavia—linked their currencies to sterling and thus formed the basis of what became known as the sterling area.

After 1945 these historical precedents for the use of sterling as a key currency were, moreover, enormously strengthened by the size of the sterling balances accumulated by India, Egypt, and other countries as a result of U.K. wartime expenditures. By the end of the war the outstanding sterling balances (about £500 million in 1939) had reached £3,500 million. Since the U.K. was unable immediately to repay these debts, they represented a vast increase in sterling held as reserves by overseas countries. During the post-war period there were large changes in the holders, and in the composition, of these sterling balances, but their level remained high (net U.K. liabilities to sterling area countries averaging about £2,500 million in the 1960s). This, in itself, necessarily made sterling a major international currency.

This factor continued to be augmented by Britain's still considerable—though relatively still further diminished—importance in world trade and finance. The anxiety of the City to maintain and extend London's role as a centre of international finance was, indeed, frequently used as an argument for, and justification of, sterling serving as a key international currency. None the less it seems probable that the U.K.'s external position was greatly weakened by the decision taken to preserve sterling as a reserve currency. Largely this was because this reserve currency function encouraged and magnified the periodic speculation against sterling which was a recurrent feature of the post-war international economy.[20]

20. It has been argued that much of this speculation would have been removed if the exchange rate had been more flexible. For most of the 1950s and 1960s, however, a flexible exchange rate for sterling was not a practical political possibility.

There are perhaps three main reasons why Britain's external position was weakened because sterling acted as a reserve currency in the international economy. Firstly, there was a strong temptation, at times when the British balance of payments was unfavourable, for holders of sterling to sell. Such selling avoided the danger of their assets being reduced by a sterling devaluation, but it also naturally contributed to any pressure against the pound. Secondly, when countries which held their reserves in sterling were themselves in deficit they were likely to finance this by running down their sterling balances. This could induce a weakening of sterling even though the current British balance of payments gave no occasion for alarm. The third reason arises simply because the sterling balances (representing a short-term liability for Britain) were so high. Their total was consistently several times greater than Britain's reserves of gold and convertible currencies, and thus there was always a psychological feeling in other countries that Britain's position was precarious.

The sterling commitment, moreover, necessarily affected economic policies from time to time. In several of the post-war crises (1949, 1955, and 1957) the deterioration in the balance of payments on current account was comparatively mild in relation to the violent speculative reactions that were produced. Thus the existence of sterling balances and sterling's role as a reserve currency sometimes necessitated internal economic policies more restrictive than would have been justifiable simply from the U.K. trading position. These considerations certainly added substantially to the reluctance to seek a solution through devaluation. Many would argue that such external constraints on government policies were salutary in themselves. And against any costs or disadvantages which these might entail would have to be set the substantial earnings of London as an international financial centre. The presumption here is that those earnings only arose because sterling was a reserve currency, but it is far from certain that all—or even most—of the services which the City performed for overseas countries were dependent upon this condition.

Of course, few of these considerations would carry much weight if Britain's overall balance had been strongly favourable—if the current balance had been sufficient to finance military expenditures overseas, net investment abroad, and perhaps also to reduce the level of Britain's short-term financial liabilities. But this was not the case. In the conditions which actually obtained, it is arguable that much of Britain's difficulty stemmed from the fact that it was (given the size of the sterling balances and the historical tradition) virtually unavoidable that sterling should be a major international currency, while (given the war-enforced sale of overseas investments) it was highly unlikely that she would have an external balance that would be large enough to fulfil such a role comfortably. That is, sterling's key position in international finance was perhaps no longer justified by Britain's position in world trade and might be beyond the long-run capacity of the economy to sustain. Not that this discomforting situation had in any sense to be imposed on Britain: indeed, the City especially had insisted upon the vital importance of sterling continuing to serve as a key international currency, and this view had been generally endorsed by post-war governments. But a desire to embrace our chains does not necessarily prevent them from being chains.

(e) *The problem of international liquidity.* The strains which were imposed upon the British economy because sterling was a major international currency were compounded by the existence of more general problems of international finance. In particular, there was a growing concern through the fifties and sixties that the growth of international trade would be seriously threatened by the inadequacy of international monetary liquidity.

There is no single international currency. In its absence countries maintain international liquid assets—that is, assets which will be readily accepted by other countries. Basically international liquidity refers to the amount, and the distribution, of these reserves—mainly, in this period, gold and foreign exchange—held by all the countries in the international economy.

The *need* for liquidity stems fundamentally from the part it plays in facilitating and promoting world trade. Trade between countries requires some means of effecting the necessary financial settlements. There are, moreover, strong advantages in encouraging trade along multilateral lines since this allows the traders of every country to buy and sell in whichever foreign market offers the best terms. Multilateral trade, however, requires sufficient financial liquidity to enable the various bilateral deficits and surpluses either to work themselves out, or to be dealt with on a national or international basis.

Other things being equal, then, a growth in world trade requires a growth in international liquidity. There was thus widespread disquiet from around the mid-1950s because it was believed that international liquidity was not growing as rapidly as world trade. It was feared that the remarkable expansion in international trade which had taken place since 1950—trade in these years was increasing at twice the rate that had been achieved between 1880 and 1913—might be jeopardised because of the inadequacy of reserves to finance it. The anxiety was all the greater because the buoyancy of trade had been an important contributory factor to the rapid economic growth of a number of countries during these years.

As already mentioned, the chief sources of reserves in the 1950s and 1960s were holdings of gold and foreign exchange. Total reserves (as Table 6.1 shows) just about doubled between 1949 and 1969, but in the same period the volume of world trade more than trebled and its value increased some four-fold.[21]

Table 6.1 **Main sources of international financial reserves**

| | In billions of (U.S.) dollars | | |
	1949	1958	1969
Gold holdings	33·3	38·1	39·1
Foreign exchange	11·2	17·1	31·9
Gross position in I.M.F.	7·9	9·8	23·7
Total	52·4	65·0	94·7

Source: I.M.F., *International Financial Statistics.*

There were several limitations on the expansion of world monetary reserves. The production of the chief traditional source of reserves, gold, grew relatively slowly—partly because the dollar price of gold had been unchanged since the 1930s. In addition, industrial uses absorbed a substantial proportion of new gold output, so that there was little additional gold available for monetary purposes. Reserves in the form of foreign exchange increased much more rapidly (in 1949 foreign exchange holdings constituted one-fifth of total reserves: by 1969 they constituted over one-third). These mainly took the form of dollars and, to a proportionately decreasing extent, sterling held by other countries. The growth of such reserves was, however, subject to a basic and increasingly severe restraint: the holders of dollars and pounds were in effect extending credit to the United

21. Bank for International Settlements, *Thirty-ninth Annual Report*, 1969, pp. 76–7.

States and the United Kingdom. Their willingness to do so ultimately rested upon the confidence they had in the stability of these currencies.

As we have seen, a shaky external confidence in sterling has been a more or less permanent post-war feature: partly for this reason sterling balances—and hence the contribution of sterling to international monetary reserves—hardly increased at all in the two decades before 1970. The position was rather different for the United States. The growth in dollar reserves held by other countries arose mainly out of overall U.S. balance of payments deficits: but the longer those deficits ran uncorrected, the more the confidence of foreign holders in the underlying stability of the dollar was brought into question. For most of the 1950s the dollar commanded complete confidence. Foreign holdings of dollars were more than adequately backed by the gold reserves of the United States. In the 1960s, however, the size and persistence of America's external deficits made other countries less willing to hold dollars. There was a tendency for some countries, particularly France, to convert their dollar holdings into gold, thus depleting America's gold reserves.

The problem is that, with fixed exchange rates, the use of a few key currencies as a major source of international liquidity rests on a basic paradox. Overall balance of payments deficits by these key currency countries are essential to secure growing international monetary reserves: but ultimately confidence in these key currencies requires that they should correct their external deficits. The dilemma thus posed emerged with increasing starkness during the 1960s. Pressures then increased for the United States (and to a lesser degree Britain) to reduce or reverse her deficits; if the United States authorities had been successful, however, the result would have been to reduce international monetary reserves at a time when there was increasing anxiety at their inadequacy.

International liquidity could have been increased in various other ways. For example, an increase in the dollar price of gold would have automatically increased the value of gold reserves. Or the need to hold reserves could have been greatly reduced if there had been no commitment to maintain a fixed exchange value: hence a general adoption of freely fluctuating exchange rates would have had the same effect as an increase in monetary reserves. All such possibilities, however, carried with them various disadvantages, often of a political nature, which prevented their adoption during this period. Instead the solution was mainly sought by increasing the reserves made available through the International Monetary Fund.

Each member country, on joining the I.M.F., is assigned a quota related in size to its importance in world trade and finance. One quarter of the quota is normally subscribed in gold and the remainder in the member's own currency. In return any member when in balance of payments difficulties can—under certain conditions and to an amount related to its quota—buy the foreign currency it needs from the Fund using its own currency for this purpose. The I.M.F. arrangements thus clearly contribute to international liquidity, which grows whenever agreements are reached for general increases in quotas. Until 1959 quotas stood at only just over $9 billion. They were increased by about 50 per cent in 1959, a further 25 per cent in 1965, and by over a third in 1970. These increases, together with the quotas for new members and other adjustments, brought the total to nearly $29 billion. In addition a supplement to the Fund's resources was provided by the so-called General Agreement to Borrow (G.A.B.), established in 1962, whereby ten leading industrial countries (the so-called Group of Ten) undertook to provide temporary loans to the I.M.F. when required.

In some respects, however, the most significant step was the introduction, in January 1970, of special drawing rights (S.D.R.s). The S.D.R.s are international monetary assets which can be used between central banks, either directly or through the Fund. The details of the operation of the scheme need not concern us; its significance is two-fold. The S.D.R.s represent a move towards the creation of a new international monetary unit and are intended to be as acceptable to the central bank as gold. They also represent an attempt to provide for a more automatic expansion of international liquidity since they could be increased by a given amount or percentage each year (the initial scheme provided for the creation of $3·5 billion worth of S.D.R.s in 1970 and a further $3 billion in each of the years 1971 and 1972).[22] In addition the effective devaluation of the U.S. dollar in 1971 was significant. It led to a generally less rigid attitude towards fixed exchange rates and to a greater willingness to consider alternative ways of increasing international liquidity.

22. The creation of the S.D.R.s could be seen as a partial vindication of the position taken by Lord Keynes, as British representative, at the time of the original discussions which led to the formation of the I.M.F. Keynes had proposed the creation of a body which would have acted much more like an international central bank, and also of an entirely new international currency called Bancor. At the time this was rejected in favour of the more cautious and restrictive American scheme, proposed by Harry White.

Whether these expectations are realised or not, it is clear that for the first quarter of a century after the Second World War there was a continuing and increasing anxiety that the growth of world trade would be endangered by an inadequate rate of increase of international liquidity. Britain was closely affected both as a major trading nation and as a provider of one source of liquidity. The attempts to maintain confidence in sterling as an international currency imposed significant restraints on British economic policy.

Other problems

It may be that the causes of the shortcomings of British economic performance lay deeper than the manifold causes so far examined, that these were, indeed, only symptoms of a more fundamental malaise. Thus it may be that the inadequate level of investment reflected a lack of faith by the British people in their own future; or that the low growth rates arose because society placed a high valuation on security and subconsciously rejected the, often unsettling, adjustments necessary for rapid economic growth.

Or, as one writer has recently tried to establish, perhaps the problems all stemmed from a fundamental deterioration in the British character which set in after 1945.[23] Or perhaps they sprang from a post-imperial torpor. The primary issues, that is to say, may well have been matters of national attitudes and character and motivation. But in our present state of knowledge such forces largely defy the kind of analysis and quantification which would allow of any reasonably objective assessment. This must be the justification for confining attention in this book mainly to the—perhaps less fundamental—economic causes of Britain's problems in the post-war world.

23. P. Einzig, *Decline and Fall? Britain's Crisis in the Sixties*, 1969.

Some suggestions for further reading

The present volume has offered a basic outline of the development of the British economy since 1919. Those readers who wish to fill in the details and enhance their knowledge of this subject will find *The Development of the British Economy, 1914–1967* by S. Pollard to be a full, informative, and reliable guide. Another book which explicitly —but more briefly—covers this period is *The British Economy, 1920–1966* by A. J. Youngson. This contains a useful discussion of the relationship between economic thought and policy in the inter-war years.

Many books exist which can provide a background to this period. Two recent examples which are both reliable and stimulating are *The First Industrial Nation: an Economic History of Britain, 1700–1914* by P. Mathias and, on a wider basis, *The Unbound Prometheus: Technological Change and Industrial Development in Western Europe since 1750* by D. S. Landes. Two other books which clearly and carefully provide both a background and a coverage of part of the period are *An Economic History of England, 1870–1939* and *A Short History of the International Economy, 1850–1950* both by W. Ashworth. D. H. Aldcroft and H. W. Richardson, *The British Economy, 1870–1939* is more difficult but contains several useful specialised articles.

The inter-war years used to be a neglected period of British history but this has rapidly changed in recent years. Besides the books already mentioned, *Britain between the Wars, 1918–1940* by C. L. Mowat excellently combines a general political account with much social and economic information. A more specialised account concentrating upon the external trading situation is *Great Britain in the World Economy* by A. E. Kahn, while the economic problems of the 1930s have been fully—if rather technically—surveyed in H. W. Richardson, *Economic Recovery in Britain, 1932–39*. There are also several good studies of specific issues, such as D. E. Moggridge, *The Return to Gold, 1925* and R. Skidelsky, *Politicians and the Slump: the Labour Government 1929–31*.

A good survey of the impact of the Second World War is contained in *British War Economy* by W. K. Hancock and M. M. Gowing. Disappointment over Britain's economic growth since 1945 has given rise to an enormous literature, most of which is either highly technical or highly ephemeral or both. The most authoritative is probably *Britain's Economic Prospects* edited by R. E. Caves, but this contains much difficult analysis. Equally illuminating and much more manageable in the area which it covers—mainly government policy—is S. Brittan, *Steering the Economy: the role of the Treasury*. A lucid and lively attempt to indicate guide-lines to assist the understanding of economic developments over the last generation or so is given in *Keynes and After* by M. Stewart, whilst *Sterling and British Policy* by Susan Strange examines the difficulties which have arisen because of the use of sterling as an international currency.

Index